Acid Rain

ACID RAIN

Eileen Lucas

Education Consultant
Helen J. Challand, Ph.D.
Professor of Science Education, National-Louis University

Acid Rain Consultant
Harriet Stubbs, Ph.D.
Director, Acid Rain Foundation

CHILDRENS PRESS ®
CHICAGO

A production of B&B Publishing, Inc.

Project Editor: Jean Blashfield Black
Designer: Elizabeth B. Graf
Computer Makeup: Dori Bechtel
Cover Design: Margrit Fiddle
Artist: Valerie A. Valusek

Photo Researcher: Terri Willis
Research Assistant: Marjorie Benson
Research Consultant: Colleen Shine
Production Assistant: Dave Conant

Printed on Evergreen Gloss
50% recycled preconsumer waste
Binder's board made from 100% recycled material

Library of Congress Cataloging-in-Publication Data

Lucas, Eileen
    Acid Rain / by Eileen Lucas.
        p. cm. -- (Saving planet Earth)
    Includes index.
    Summary: Discusses the causes and harmful effects of acid rain and examines
possible solutions for this pollution problem.
    ISBN 0-516-05503-8
    1. Acid rain — Environmental aspects — Juvenile literature. 2. Air Pollution
— Juvenile literature. [1. Acid rain. 2. Air Pollution. 3. Pollution.] I. Title.
II. Series.
TD195.44.L83   1991
363.73'86--dc20
                                                 91-3879
                                                     CIP
                                                         AC

Cover photo—© Imtek Imagineering/Masterfile

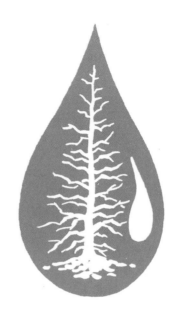

TABLE OF CONTENTS

Chapter 1

Forever Wild

AS THE SUN RISES over Adirondack Park in New York State on a warm spring morning, the tree-covered mountains are smothered in clouds. The snow, which has piled up all winter, is beginning to melt. The air is full of moisture, and streams flow swiftly down the mountainsides, carrying the melted snow to lakes and rivers in the valley below.

The sun rises higher and shines on a clear, silver-blue mountain lake. Gradually, the clouds lift a little, and all is silent and peaceful.

What is wrong with this picture? At first glance—nothing. A visitor would see a great wilderness hideaway, a place far from the pollution-causing activities of humans. Nearly 2½ million acres (1 million hectares) of the 6 million acres (2.4 million hectares) making up Adirondack Park are owned by the state of New York. And the state constitution decrees that the park shall remain "forever wild." Even the land within the park that is privately owned must be used only according to strict guidelines.

But appearances can be deceiving. In the part of Adirondack Park that remains undeveloped—where there are no roads or billboards, no tourist markers, and no campsites— we can find the telltale fingerprints of pollution. In this case, the culprit is acid rain.

A closer look at the forested peaks reveals an unusually large number of fallen trees. Also, many of the red spruce and balsam fir are bare at the top, and the lower branches have lost many needles. If you could see inside the trunks, you would notice that the growth rings for recent years are much thinner than the rings for previous decades.

Stepping up to the shore of the silver-blue lake, you

might marvel at how clear the water is. You can even see to the bottom of the lake, where leaves that fell last autumn are still lying.

But such clear water is not normal. Nor is it normal that last year's leaves are perfectly preserved, with no sign of decay. And no fish swim in the lake. An occasional insect skims across the surface, but no frog waits to gobble it up, and no bird swoops down to catch it on the wing.

The very stillness of this spring morning tells you that something is wrong, and the silence is suddenly frightening.

The wildlife of a forest area, such as these owls, can fall victim to acid rain when the food chain is broken.

The Lake Is Not Alone

The foggy mountain air, the damaged forest, and the clear, lifeless lake are all linked to the problem of acid rain. Some two hundred lakes in the Adirondacks are dead. Many acres of forests are dying. The Adirondack region, like the rest of the northern part of the Appalachian Mountains, is among those areas in the United States hardest hit by acid rain. These peaceful places are being harmed by the activities in the industrial cities where the acid pollution starts.

But this is by no means simply a regional problem. Many other parts of the United States, ranging from Florida to California to Minnesota, are also facing problems caused by pollution. It affects nearly all our cities, and many beautiful wilderness areas as well. In Canada, there are lakes where fish no longer swim. In southern Norway, about 80 percent of the lakes are dead or dying. Acid rain is a serious problem in much of the rest of Europe, too, and Germany's famous Black Forest is dying—another victim of pollution, including acid rain.

Acid rain is rain, snow, sleet, or other forms of precipitation that have a higher acid content than normal. Some acids occur naturally in the atmosphere, but many others are the result of human activities. When these acids collect in the atmosphere, they combine with moisture in the air and the result is rain that is sometimes as acid as vinegar.

Acid rain is a result of the air pollution that human activities cause, and if we want to help save planet Earth, we must begin to do something about it.

Needle loss and color change are among the noticeable effects pollutants in the air can have on conifers like these.

Chapter 2

The Fossil Fuel Connection

TO UNDERSTAND HOW acid rain is harming our planet, we need to know something about fossil fuels.

Coal, oil, and natural gas are called fossil fuels. They were formed over millions of years from the remains of once-living trees, other plants, and animals. These living things died and fell into the swamps that covered ancient Earth. Year by year, century by century, more living things fell on top of the older ones. Over millions of years, the organic (once living) material was compressed by the weight above it and was gradually changed into the fossil fuels that we now remove from the earth for use in producing energy. When these fuels are burned, the energy stored by those ancient living organisms is given off in the form of heat. This heat is converted into the energy that runs our world.

Large amounts of fossil fuels are burned at fantastically high temperatures in power plants that produce energy. For example, 600 tons (540 metric tons) of coal are burned each hour in both boilers at the plant belonging to American Electric Power Company (AEP) near Cheshire, Ohio. The temperatures in these boilers reach 3500 degrees F. (about 1942 degrees C). This heat is used to make steam that turns turbines, which produce the electricity that lights up our homes and runs our modern world.

Three mines are operated by the AEP, staffed by some 1,800 workers, just to supply this one power plant. Mountains of coal are carried on 10-mile (16-kilometer)-long conveyor belts from the mines to the power plant near the banks of the Ohio River. And even that isn't enough. Additional coal is brought in on trains and barges to feed the huge appetite of the power-generating machinery.

Coal in huge amounts (left) *is used by power plants and factories worldwide. But not all coal is alike, and much of it contains impurities such as sulfite and clay* (above).

FACT

One pound (0.45 kilogram) of coal can produce enough electricity to light ten 100-watt bulbs for an hour. Each ton (900 kilograms) of coal burned at a power plant supplies about 2,000 kilowatt-hours of electricity, about enough to supply an average house for about six weeks.

Heat Is Not All That's Produced

The heat released by fossil-fuel burning is trapped and used to boil water, which produces steam that turns electricity-generating turbines. But, unfortunately, more than heat is released in the process. All the other chemical components that were part of the coal, oil, or gas are also released, and they are generally sent up a smokestack and expelled into the air. These components are called emissions.

The major emissions from burning fossil fuels are carbon dioxide and oxides of sulfur and nitrogen. Normally, carbon dioxide would be considered a harmless emission. Human beings give off carbon dioxide with every breath. Trees and other plants take it in and use it to make their food. But today, too many trees are being cut down and too much fuel is being burned. So large quantities of carbon dioxide are building up in our atmosphere.

Carbon dioxide keeps our planet warm by trapping heat rays from the sun within the atmosphere. This process is called the *greenhouse effect*. But now there is too much carbon dioxide in the atmosphere. So the Earth is getting warmer and warmer—a process called *global warming*. Most scientists believe global warming is dangerous to life on our planet.

Emissions from Fossil Fuels

Fossil fuels are very complex substances, made up of a variety of chemical elements. Although carbon dioxide is the main emission released by burning, several other substances are also released, the ones that play the major role in the formation of acid rain.

This peculiar apparatus measures how wind picks up contaminated particles and transports them to other locations.

13

Sulfur and Nitrogen Compounds. The two main elements released by burning are sulfur and nitrogen. Sulfur combines with oxygen in the air to form sulfur dioxide (SO_2). When sulfur dioxide mixes with water vapor in the air, it becomes sulfuric acid (H_2SO_4).

When nitrogen mixes with oxygen at high temperatures, it forms one of the oxides of nitrogen, usually written NO_x. When a nitrogen oxide is exposed to water vapor, it becomes nitric acid (HNO_3).

In concentrated form, both sulfuric acid and nitric acid are very powerful substances, useful in a number of carefully controlled chemical processes. Fortunately, when these acids form in the atmosphere, they are diluted, or not at full strength. Yet we are now finding out that even in diluted form, these acids are quite capable of causing damage to our environment.

Sulfuric acid and nitric acid are the main ingredients of acid rain. Scientists call acid rain *acid deposition* because it can be either wet or dry. In its wet form, acid deposition includes acids in rain, snow, sleet, hail, and fog. In its dry form, acid deposition consists of tiny particles of sulfur and nitrogen compounds and the gases sulfur dioxide and nitrogen oxides.

There are natural sources of sulfur and nitrogen emissions, such as volcanic activity, wildfire, lightning, and gases given off by swamps. However, these sources are much less important than emissions caused by human activities. And most emissions caused by humans come from burning fossil fuels. Emissions occur at metal-smelting and power-generating plants, in motor vehicle engines, in the heating of homes and businesses, and in various industrial processes.

Air-pollution-control laws were passed in the 1970s and

An electron microscope reveals crystals of a mineral called gypsum that form when sulfuric acid in rain reacts with calcium in a leaf.

The sources of pollution that can contribute to acid rain are all around us. Some are natural, such as volcanoes (above), but most involve human activities. Power plants (below) produce the most sulfur dioxide, which becomes sulfuric acid in water vapor. Metal smelting (left) contributes. Most nitrogen oxides, which can become nitric acid, are produced by mobile sources, such as the millions of cars that crowd our highways (top left) and the trucks (bottom left) that now haul most of our cargo.

1980s, and the Clean Air Act was amended in 1990. Laws have been passed to force industry to reduce their emissions, but they need to be reduced even more—in many places, much more. Also, the major reduction so far has been in sulfur emissions, and many other toxic (harmful) emissions also need to be reduced.

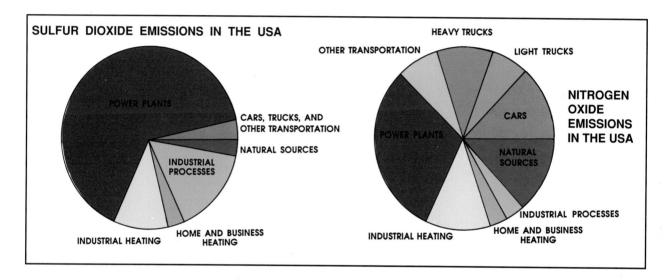

SULFUR DIOXIDE EMISSIONS IN THE USA

POWER PLANTS

CARS, TRUCKS, AND OTHER TRANSPORTATION

NATURAL SOURCES

INDUSTRIAL PROCESSES

INDUSTRIAL HEATING

HOME AND BUSINESS HEATING

HEAVY TRUCKS

OTHER TRANSPORTATION

LIGHT TRUCKS

NITROGEN OXIDE EMISSIONS IN THE USA

CARS

POWER PLANTS

NATURAL SOURCES

INDUSTRIAL PROCESSES

INDUSTRIAL HEATING

HOME AND BUSINESS HEATING

Toxic Rain. In addition to the sulfur and nitrogen compounds, up to fifty other elements may be released when fossil fuels are burned. These elements include mercury, arsenic, cadmium, aluminum, and lead, all of which can be extremely toxic. The emissions from smelters, where such metals as copper, iron, and zinc are separated from their ores, are also high in metal content.

These elements are dispersed into the atmosphere as tiny particles, often attaching themselves to bits of dust or ash in the air. They are then washed back to the Earth with the next rain or snowfall. Such precipitation is called toxic rain. Toxic rain pollutes surface waters and soils and is absorbed into the tissues of plants and animals.

Many toxic substances ride the winds, hitchhiking on dust particles in the air. Later they fall with rain or snow to pollute water and soil. Then they may be absorbed into plant and animal tissues.

Mercury has been found in the sediment of lakes in Wisconsin that are almost exclusively rain fed. The mercury may have been emitted from a smokestack somewhere, carried on the wind, and deposited with rainfall into these otherwise pure lakes. Dioxins—by-products of the manufacturing of many different pesticides and other chemicals—and other cancer-

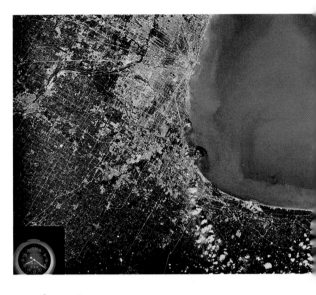

Smoke plumes (above) *reach into the sky from the many heavy industries located southeast of Chicago. The pollutants in such smoke are carried by high winds to such vulnerable areas as this wetland* (left), *which appears to have been damaged by acid rain and other air pollution.*

17

causing pollutants found in Lake Siskiwit on Isle Royale in Lake Superior have also been linked to toxic rain.

Clearly, much more than heat is given off when fossil fuels are burned. We've been using our atmosphere as a chemical dumping site. But what goes up *does* come down. And when it comes down, it may be harmful.

Acids and Bases

Sulfur and nitrogen compounds make the rain harmful because they may become acidic. The experiment below may help you understand acids, and their chemical opposites,

An Earth Experience

Testing for Acids and Bases

Litmus paper is paper that has been specially treated to determine whether substances are acidic or basic. It can be purchased from any scientific supply company, or your school science teacher would know where to get some.

Litmus paper comes in two colors—red and blue. Red litmus paper turns blue when it is moistened with a base but remains red in an acid. Blue paper is turned red by acids but remains blue in a base. If a substance is neutral, neither acidic nor basic, neither paper will change color.

which are called bases or alkalines, as well as substances that are *neutral*, neither acid nor base.

Remember, strong acids and bases can be harmful. Although the substances used in the experiment are weak, it is a good idea to carry out this and other experiments suggested in this book under adult supervision. It is also a good idea to protect your eyes with safety glasses when you are conducting an experiment. And always keep your fingers out of the solutions being tested. Some of the solutions might harm your skin, and sweat or dirt on your fingers can influence the results.

This experiment will tell you which of various household substances are acidic and which are basic. Select a variety of liquids to be tested, such as tap water, starch, salt, vinegar, hand soap, baking soda, dish detergent, shampoo, window cleaner, soft drink, milk, and fruit juice. Before you begin this experiment, dissolve the solids in a small amount of distilled water.

Make a list of the substances you have chosen to test, indicating whether you expect them to be acidic, neutral, or basic.

First, test some distilled water with both red and blue litmus paper. Probably the blue paper will stay blue and the red will stay red. This result means that the distilled water is a neutral substance, neither acidic nor basic.

Now carefully test each substance by placing a piece of litmus paper in the liquid. Use each piece of litmus paper only once. Record the results. Were there any surprises? Were any of the substances you tested neutral like the distilled water?

---

pH Values. The strength of an acid or base is measured by using the *pH scale*—"pH" stands for *potential hydrogen.* The element hydrogen is a critical factor in determining the acidity of a substance. A pH value close to 0 is usually as strong as an acid gets. A value of pH 7 means that the substance is neutral—neither acidic nor basic—and a pH close to 14 is as basic (alkaline) as a substance can be. Remember, the lower the pH value, the stronger the acid. Very few substances are truly neutral.

The pH scale, with some examples of the acidity of some common products

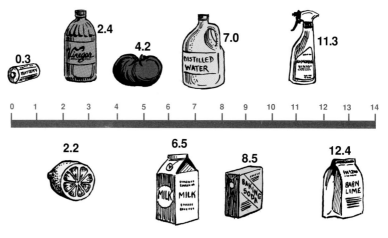

The pH scale is logarithmic. In a logarithmic scale, a change of one whole number represents an increase or decrease in the pH value by ten. For example, a substance with a pH of 5 is ten times more acidic than one with a pH of 6. A pH 4 substance is ten times more acidic than a pH 5 substance, and 100 times (10 x 10) more acidic than a pH 6 substance.

The pH of Rain

Unpolluted rain usually has a pH of about 5.0. It is somewhat acidic because carbon dioxide in the atmosphere com-

bines with water to form carbonic acid, a very mild acid. Virtually all plants and animals can neutralize the acidity in normal rainfall so it is not damaging.

However, when large quantities of certain kinds of pollutants are expelled into the air (such as oxides of sulfur and nitrogen) and acids are formed, the pH value of rainfall can drop.

Acid rain can affect the natural ability of plants and animals and their habitats to neutralize acid. When terrestrial (land) and aquatic (water) ecosystems can no longer handle the stress of the extra acidity, they lose the ability to neutralize. Then the land and water become acidic. This can be harmful, even fatal, to organisms that live in these ecosystems.

These are very complex processes. A wide variety of

Clouds in a mountain valley may contain acids that settle on the trees, lakes, and soil.

chemical reactions take place as a drop of acid rain hits a leaf and falls to the forest floor. Sometimes it takes many years of acid deposition for effects to be noticeable. We will discuss this more in the chapters dealing with the effects of acid deposition on water and on soil.

Dropping pH Values. Over the past several decades, scientists have been keeping records of the pH values of precipitation around the world. To compare the past with the present, they have also studied glacial ice dating back millions of years. They found that the amount of acid in rain was insignificant until the 1800s.

An Earth Experience

Measuring the pH of Rainfall

In this experiment you will test and record the pH of rainfall in several places near your home. You will need several jars or plastic bottles to catch the rainwater and a funnel to direct the rainwater into each jar. The jars should first be thoroughly washed with distilled water and then dried with a clean towel.

You will also need some pH measuring paper, which, like litmus paper, is available at a scientific supply company. But unlike litmus paper, pH measuring paper tells you how strong an acid or base the substance is.

Select several places to collect rainwater samples, such as near a busy highway, near a factory that has smokestacks, in an open field away from industry, and in your own backyard. You may need an adult to drive you to some locations to set your collection jars out and to pick them up after a rainfall. Record the location of each jar.

With the coming of the Industrial Revolution and the increased burning of coal and oil for fuel, people began to send many tons of acid-forming gases and particles into the air. In 1872, an Englishman named Robert Smith published a book called *Air and Rain* in which he linked emissions from coal burning to metals rusting and dyes fading in areas where there was heavy use of coal.

By the early 1900s, acid rain was affecting fish in Norwegian and Swedish lakes. It wasn't until the 1960s, however, that a Swedish scientist, Svante Oden, pointed out that the acidity of Scandinavian lakes had been affected by pollution carried on the wind from Great Britain and Western Europe.

Collect your samples as soon after a rain as possible. Test and record the pH of each with pH measuring paper. Do some samples register as more acidic than others? What factors at each site might account for your findings?

Repeat this experiment several times. Even the beginning of a rainstorm may be more acidic than the end. Are there changes in the pH level of rain in any of the locations you've chosen? You might want to see if there are any individuals or agencies monitoring pH levels in your area. Do your findings agree with theirs? Has there been a pattern of increased or decreased pH levels in your area over time?

Field technicians check wind and rain gauges near a power plant as part of the process of testing for acid rain.

In the 1960s a Canadian scientist who was working in England linked the sulfur and nitrogen compounds in polluted air to an increase in respiratory illness in British cities. Other scientists in Britain began recording rainfall with pH values a hundred times more acidic than normal. In places across the Northern Hemisphere, the acid content of the air was increasing.

During this period, concern about acid rain grew in the

FACT

Readings of pH 2.4—as acidic as vinegar—were recorded during some storms in New England. During one particularly acid summer storm, rain falling on a lime-green automobile leached away the yellow in the green paint, leaving blue raindrop-shaped spots on the car.

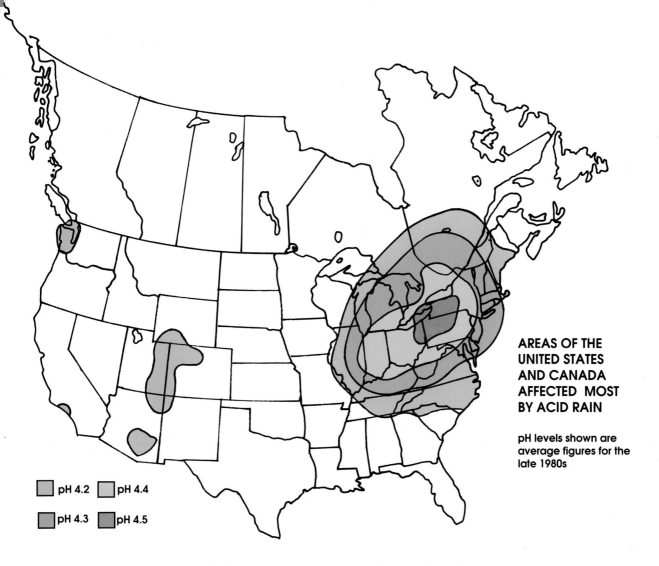

AREAS OF THE
UNITED STATES
AND CANADA
AFFECTED MOST
BY ACID RAIN

pH levels shown are
average figures for the
late 1980s

pH 4.2 pH 4.4

pH 4.3 pH 4.5

United States as well. Scientists measuring the acidity of rainfall east of the Mississippi River began getting frequent readings well below the normal pH of rain. In the New England states, these readings were often as low as 3.8 in the summer. In 1979, the average reading for rainfall in the area including Ontario in Canada and New York and Pennsylvania in the United States was pH 4.1. As of 1990, rainfall in the eastern United States had an average pH value of 4.2, much more acidic than normal, unpolluted rain would be.

Chapter 3

The Culprits
in the Case of Acid Rain

AS SCIENTIFIC REPORTS on acid rain were made public, people in many countries became alarmed. They wondered what was causing this problem and what could be done about it. The answer is complicated, but basically, acid rain is caused by the increasing amounts of sulfur and nitrogen compounds discharged into the air.

Approximately 35 million tons (31.5 million metric tons) of sulfur dioxide and 24 million tons (22 million metric tons) of nitrogen oxides are sent into the atmosphere each year over North America (including Canada and Mexico as well as the United States). Many researchers predict that emissions levels will continue to rise through the 1990s and into the twenty-first century.

Over half the sulfur dioxide comes from power plants that burn coal to make electricity. Most of us don't think much about where electric power comes from. We take it for granted that when we turn on an electric light or a TV set, it will work. But the electricity that runs these appliances has to come from somewhere. And in many cases, that "somewhere" is a huge power plant where tons of coal are burned.

There are more power plants in the eastern half of the United States than in the West. The majority are in the states bordering the Great Lakes and the Ohio River Valley. But just about anywhere in the world where there are large cities, there are power plants. And where there are power plants that burn fossil fuels, there are emissions of sulfur dioxide and nitrogen oxides—and acid rain.

Power plants are just one of the types of places where fossil fuels are burned, however. Many manufacturing processes, such as the making of automobiles, paper, and

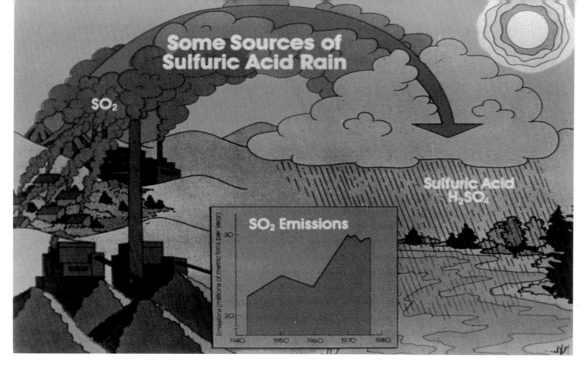

The graphs above and below show that the emission of sulfur dioxide and nitrogen oxides increased as the human activities of energy production and transportation increased, primarily because of the increased use of fossil fuels.

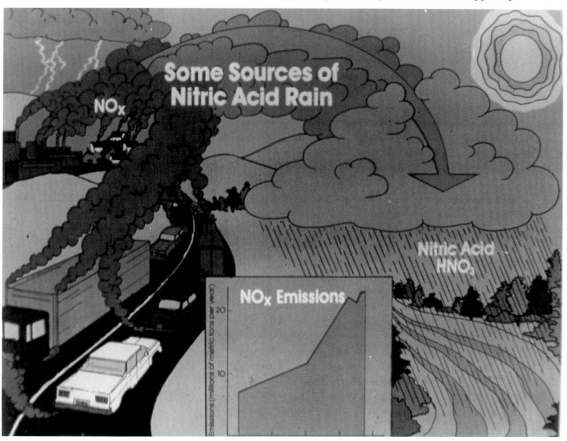

chemicals, require heat. This heat comes from burning fossil fuels in industrial boilers. The smokestacks of these boilers are a significant source of acid rain.

Another major source of nitrogen and sulfur emissions is vehicle engines. Cars, trucks, buses, trains, and airplanes all run on fuel, and when fuel is used, pollutants are emitted. Also, the fossil fuel that we burn to heat homes and businesses and to operate household and business tools adds pollutants to the air.

Reviewing Your Own Use of Fossil Fuels

An Earth Experience

The major use of fossil fuel is in the making of electricity. Think about all the ways you use electricity in your home. Go from room to room and make a list of all your electrical appliances. You might be surprised at how many there are.

What would happen if you had to go without electricity for a few hours, or a few days? How would it affect your life? Find out where the power plant that supplies your electricity is located and what kind of fuel it burns.

Now consider the types of fuel used by your family. Besides all the electricity used, there may be other fuels used for such household tasks as cooking, heating, and drying clothes. How many cars does your family have and what kind of fuel do they burn? How often do you use other forms of transportation? What about fuel burned in outdoor appliances such as lawn mowers, grills, and chainsaws. Don't forget recreational vehicles such as motorbikes, jet skis, boats, and snowmobiles.

Where do these fuels come from? You probably found that most fuels you use come from coal, oil, and natural gas.

Although most people are aware of the problem of acid rain, many miners see coal as the only reasonable energy source.

Ore-smelting plants are another major user of fossil fuels. Valuable minerals, such as iron, copper, and silver are separated from their ores in such plants. This process requires a great deal of heat, which is supplied by burning fossil fuels—mainly coal.

In Sudbury, Ontario, Canada, sulfur and nitrogen emissions from ore smelting have created extremely serious environmental and health problems. But concerned people are trying to solve these problems.

The Story of Sudbury

The area around Sudbury, Ontario, has been described by Thomas Pawlick, author of *A Killing Rain*, as "more sinister than Tolkien's Land of Mordor where the shadows lie." It looks so much like the moon that American astronauts have been sent there on training missions. This barren landscape is the result of emissions from an ore-smelting plant. It was sending twice as much sulfur into the air as the volcano, Mount St. Helens, did in the year it polluted the air most.

In 1886, the International Nickel Company (Inco) began mining and smelting nickel (a strong and useful metal) near Sudbury. At first they used a method called heat roasting, in which raw ore was placed on a bed of blazing wood. There it would smolder for months until the metal was free from the rock. During the early 1900s, the process was made more efficient. But none of the improvements decreased the heavy black clouds of smoke produced in the smelting process.

Instead, as efficiency improved, more ore was burned and the black smoke got thicker. By the 1960s, farmers in the area had gone bankrupt—crops would no longer grow in the fields of Sudbury. Neither would trees nor grass nor even weeds. As the vegetation died, the soil began to erode, leaving bare, blackened rock. The paint on houses and cars peeled, and workers and their families suffered from lung and skin diseases.

In 1970, pressure from environmental groups forced the government to demand that Inco cut down its emissions. At that time, the plant was spitting out some 6,000 tons (5,400 metric tons) of sulfur dioxide a day. It was ordered to reduce

The sulfur in the thick black smoke produced by the Inco plant at Sudbury, Ontario, created this barren landscape.

The Superstack on the Copper Cliff smelter at Sudbury, Ontario, is now the tallest smokestack in the world.

that to 5,200 tons (4,700 metric tons) a day right away. The emissions had to drop further to 3,600 tons (3,200 metric tons) a day within six years.

Part of the reduction came from the added process of "cleaning" the sulfur from the nickel ore before it was put through the smelter. But the company decided that the best way to protect Sudbury from pollution was to build a taller smokestack. The new stack that the company built rose 1,250 feet (375 meters) in the air, taller than any other smokestack in the world. Called the Superstack, it released the poisonous emissions higher up in the atmosphere, so that the air around the Sudbury area was indeed cleaner. But what happened to the emissions?

At first it was hoped that the gases emitted from the Inco Superstack would blend with the air of the upper atmosphere and just go away. But pollution never really goes "away"—it just goes somewhere else. And that somewhere else was downwind from Sudbury.

The area downwind from Sudbury is one of the most beautiful parts of Canada. Located 50 miles (80 kilometers) to the southwest is the Killarney Lakes region. Artists once came from all over Canada to paint its lovely scenic landscapes. But since the 1960s scientists have come from all over the world to study its acidified lakes and soils.

Before the Superstack was built, scientists found that

soils within 20 to 30 miles (32 to 48 kilometers) downwind of Sudbury were polluted by acid rain and loaded with toxic metals (which had been both deposited from the sky and released from the soil). Consequently, they were depleted of beneficial nutrients.

When the Superstack began operating, the same damage was discovered even farther downwind, hundreds of miles away.

After years of acidic rainfall with pH levels of 4 and below, the pH readings of lakes in the area began to fall, too. Snow with equally low pH melted into these lakes each spring. New generations of fish were nonexistent because the fish eggs did not develop and many mature fish became unable to lay eggs.

Nellie Lake in the La Cloche Mountains has become acidified by acid deposition resulting from emissions coming from the Inco Superstack.

The destruction spread throughout other beautiful cottage areas of Ontario, such as the Muskoka-Haliburton region. These areas are caught between pollution carried on the air from Sudbury and pollution brought from the north-central United States. No matter which way the wind blows, they get dumped on.

Tourism is one of Ontario's largest sources of income, bringing in about $5 billion annually and providing some 470,000 jobs. Areas that depend on tourists would be devastated without visitors. But who would want to visit an acidified lake or an acidified forest where hazy, polluted air spoils the view, where fish are unsafe to eat (if they can be found at all), and where the sounds of loons and croaking frogs have been stilled?

In the meantime, many cottages have been closed up, and

Until the Inco smelters began to emit less pollutant, the barren ground did not have a chance to recover.

countless fishing poles are gathering dust in attics and closets.

But the people of Ontario are responding. They are asking their government to do something about the emissions coming from Sudbury, from other Canadian industries, and from American sources as well. They are also conserving energy, such as by recycling as much as possible.

And to some extent, their voices are being heard. In January 1989, Inco announced a $494-million pollution-control program to further reduce sulfur dioxide emissions. Oxygen flash furnaces—a new technology that does not burn fossil fuels—will be used.

Even more important, however, is the fact that in March 1991, the United States and Canada signed an Agreement on Air Quality. It commits the United States to preventing 2 million tons (1.8 million metric tons) of nitrogen oxide emis-

sions above the level emitted in 1980 from entering the air. It also cuts 10 million tons (9 million metric tons) of sulfur dioxide emissions by the year 2000. In addition, American power plants must limit their sulfur dioxide emissions by the year 2010. That means that they will have to find alternate sources of energy for creating electricity or cleaner ways to burn coal.

The United States is not alone in having to take action, however. Canada will also have to cut its sulfur dioxide emissions by 2.3 million tons (2 million metric tons) by 1994. This will have a beneficial effect on the acid rain levels in the Adirondack Mountains, which gets polluted air from both Canada and the United States.

President George Bush said on signing the agreement, "Pollution is never stopped by a line on a map. Transboundary pollution [which crosses borders between countries] requires cooperative global stewardship among all nations."

The same area seen on the previous page seven years after the reduction in emissions and the treatment of the land began.

Chapter 4

Five Factors:
From Emissions
to Effects

ACID RAIN IS REALLY A SERIES of interactions and reactions among various factors in the environment and society. A thorough study of acid rain involves history, economics, politics, geography, geology, meteorology, and even more. To better understand the problem, we can trace it through five stages: emission, transport, transformation, deposition, and effects.

Emissions deals with the source of the pollutant—what is released into the air—and where. *Transport* deals with how these pollutants are carried through the air from the point of emission to the point of deposit. *Transformation* describes what happens to the pollutants while they are in the air. *Deposition* describes the ways in which the pollutants fall to earth and the kinds of environmental surfaces they come in contact with. And *effects* are what happens after deposition.

Emissions

Throughout the 1960s, sulfur dioxide emissions were on the increase, reaching a peak of about 31 million tons (28 million metric tons) per year around 1970. During this same time period, awareness of this environmental problem was growing. Government and industry began to react to public concern, and sulfur dioxide emissions began to drop in many areas. By 1985, about 23 million tons (20.7 million metric tons) were still being emitted into the air in the United States. Over half of that came from the ten-state area of Illinois, Indiana, Kentucky, Michigan, Missouri, New York, Ohio, Pennsylvania, Tennessee, and West Virginia. Significant levels of sulfur dioxide emissions have also been registered in the Southeast and West. So virtually every region of the nation is contributing to this form of pollution.

An atmospheric sampling tower located near Clingman's Dome in the Great Smoky Mountains. Measurements of atmospheric chemistry and weather are taken so that their effects on the mountain spruce forests can be studied.

Since then, sulfur dioxide emissions have continued to drop slowly. By 1990, slight improvements were continuing to be made, but we still had a long way to go.

Nitrogen oxides are a different story. Like sulfur dioxide, these emissions were also increasing in the United States during the 1960s. But after reaching a level of about 18 million tons (16 million metric tons) in 1970, nitrogen oxides emission levels continued to increase. By 1980, they were up to about 21 million tons (18.9 million metric tons). Automobile pollution control efforts in the early 1980s helped somewhat. The 1985 figure for nitrogen oxides emissions was a little under 19 million tons (17 million metric tons). Since the single largest source of nitrogen oxide pollution is motor vehicles, which are just about everywhere, these emissions are found throughout North America. As the number of automobiles in use throughout the world continues to rise, the nitrogen oxide emissions also rise.

Advances in emissions controls are making headway around the world. Other countries are bringing their emissions levels down. They enforce laws that forbid high levels of emissions and they use high-tech controls on smokestacks. In Sweden, emissions of sulfur dioxide and other pollutants have been reduced by 75 percent. As of 1989, West Germany had cut sulfur dioxide emissions by 90 percent. Germany will have a difficult time, however, bringing factories and power plants built in East Germany under Communist domination up to West German standards. Eastern European countries will have a tough time cutting emissions as they try to improve their economies at the same time.

Transport

Lakes in upstate New York are polluted with acids that came from power plants in the Midwest. How can this be?

When emissions leave smokestacks and exhaust pipes, two things can happen. Either they settle fairly close to the place where they were emitted (*short-range transport*), or they are carried high up into the air where they become part of vast weather systems that can cover hundreds of miles a day

A specially equipped airplane is used to monitor the long-range transport of pollutants.

The clarity and blue color of this lake make it quite beautiful to look at, but these traits can be symptoms of a lake that has become acidified by acid rain.

(*long-range transport*). Emissions from Chicago can wind up—or rain down—in Montreal, Canada, within three days.

Weather systems across central and eastern North America generally travel from west to east and may cover 300 to 500 miles (480 to 800 kilometers) a day. If particles can remain aloft for up to a week—as scientists have shown they can—they could travel quite a long way. For example, 300 miles (480 kilometers) a day for two days would mean a trip of 600 miles (960 kilometers). And 500 miles (800 kilometers) a day for four days could carry a batch of emissions 2,000 miles (3,200 kilometers)!

Factors such as air temperature, wind speed, and the terrain affect the distance that emissions can travel. In the summer when air is warmer, emissions often stay closer to their source. At night and in the winter when air is cooler, they tend to travel farther.

Smokestacks Make a Global Problem. Unfortunately, the transport of acid and toxic particles became a bigger problem *after* efforts were made to clean up the air in certain areas of dense pollution. In the late 1960s, air-quality standards were set for industries that were polluting heavily. In order to meet these standards, many polluters, like Inco, built taller smokestacks, or tallstacks. It seemed reasonable to believe that emissions sent higher into the air would disperse harmlessly in the upper atmosphere. We know from the Sudbury experience how wrong this belief turned out to be. But the damage was already done.

Prior to the 1960s, most smokestacks were about 200 feet (61 meters) tall. This was only high enough to send emissions into local weather systems, which usually meant that pollutants were deposited within 20 to 30 miles (32 to 48 kilometers) of the source. But with the coming of tallstacks in the late 1960s and early 1970s, the height of the average smokestack rose to over 700 feet (210 meters), with several towering more than 1,000 feet (300 meters) in the air.

Smokestacks, tallstacks, and the Superstack—all are ways of sending smoke and its pollutants into the atmosphere.

To make matters worse, gases burst out of these monstrous stacks at speeds that sometimes exceed 50 miles (80 kilometers) per hour. At these speeds, emissions often shoot up to twice the stack's height. At those heights, gases become part of weather systems that reach far beyond local, state, and national borders.

The Gavin Power Plant in Cheshire, Ohio, has a tallstack that reaches 1,103 feet (340 meters). The Inco Superstack in Sudbury, Ontario, is the tallest in the world. At 1,250 feet (384 meters), it is as tall as the Empire State Building in New York City.

FACT

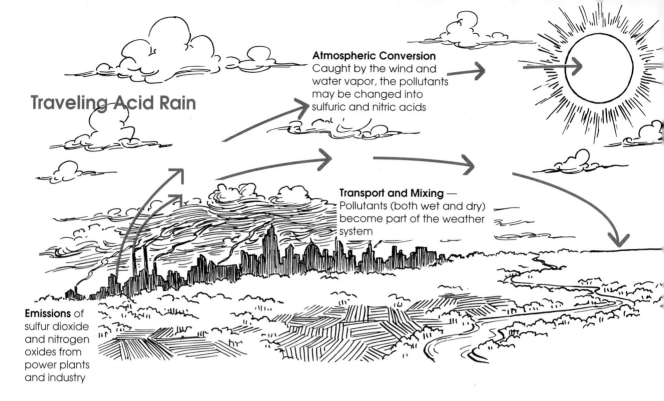

Traveling Acid Rain

Atmospheric Conversion
Caught by the wind and water vapor, the pollutants may be changed into sulfuric and nitric acids

Transport and Mixing — Pollutants (both wet and dry) become part of the weather system

Emissions of sulfur dioxide and nitrogen oxides from power plants and industry

Sulfur and nitrogen emissions from the United States find their way into Canada and vice versa, depending on which way the wind is blowing at any particular time. Both U.S. and Canadian studies agree that the United States sends three or four times more sulfur dioxide into Canada than Canada sends to the United States. In other words, the two countries both import and export acid rain, but the United States exports much more than Canada does.

Sulfur and nitrogen emissions from Western Europe and Britain travel to the Scandinavian countries. Emissions from Central and Eastern Europe and the Soviet Union are deposited on Arctic snow.

Scientists have reported pollutants traveling thousands of miles across oceans and continents. In 1991, the Persian Gulf war ended in March, with almost a thousand oil wells left burning in Kuwait. By May the pollution from those fires had traveled around the world in the upper atmosphere and

Wet Deposition of sulfuric and nitric acids occurs at long distances when the acids mix with rain, snow, sleet, and clouds

Dry Deposition of sulfur and nitrogen as gas or particles usually occurs close to the source

was showing up in haze and red sunsets in the Far East. With such transport, it is easy to see why acid rain has become a global problem.

Transformation

The third stage of the pollution process is tricky—sort of a wild-card situation in which it's hard to be sure exactly what will happen. The chemicals we put into the atmosphere have turned the air we breathe into a sort of "soup." Many different chemical reactions are going on all the time. The different types and amounts of chemicals affect these reactions, as does the amount of moisture in the air, the temperature, and the presence of clouds or sunshine.

As soon as sulfur and nitrogen gases are emitted,

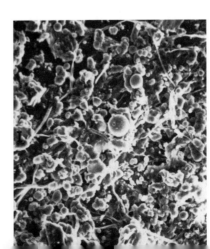

This is a greatly enlarged view of particles of pollutants deposited on leaves in a forest. The round particles are ash from a power plant. They contain a number of toxic metals that may damage the leaves.

43

When air pollutants have killed the trees in a forest, there are no living roots to hold the soil to the subsurface rock, and so it erodes away.

they are transformed into sulfur dioxide and nitrogen oxides. That's one transformation. The longer these gases stay in the air, the more likely they are to come in contact with water vapor. Then another chemical reaction happens, and this time the gases turn into sulfuric and nitric acid.

Tallstacks make the situation worse. Emissions sent high into the sky tend to stay in the air longer, giving them more time to react with other chemicals and form even more dangerous substances.

Dry sulfur and nitrogen particles that are deposited fairly quickly—before chemically combining with water—are not always harmless either. Transformation can take place after these pollutants have settled on vegetation or the ground. If they happen to fall into a body of water—even a puddle—or if they settle on a leaf or a building and then rain falls, they can still become damaging sulfuric or nitric acid.

Ozone. It is during the transformation stage that many *secondary pollutants* are formed. These are chemical compounds that were not present in the original emissions (the *primary* pollutants). They form from reactions between the various pollutants and the gases and other substances that are naturally present in the atmosphere. One of the most damaging secondary pollutants is ozone (O$_3$).

The confusing thing about ozone is that when it is high in the Earth's atmosphere, it is stratospheric ozone, a beneficial substance. It helps protect the Earth from dangerous ultraviolet rays of the sun. But when it is formed in the lower atmosphere—in the air we breathe—it is tropospheric ozone, which can be very dangerous.

Tropospheric ozone is formed by reactions between nitrogen oxides and hydrocarbons (petroleum-based chemicals) in the presence of sunshine. It is the main chemical in smog. Too much ozone in the air makes breathing difficult, especially for older persons, young children, and people with asthma. Prolonged exposure can lead to heart and lung disease, even death. Though ozone is formed in cities, it causes billions of dollars in crop losses on farms each year. It is also believed to be important in forest decline and death.

Ozone is a secondary pollutant formed from gasoline exhaust acted on by sunlight. As transportation in Third World countries becomes increasingly centered around the automobile, pollution problems will increase.

Scientists studying the deposition of acids in snow may have to reach their study area—such as this remote lake in the mountains—by helicopter.

Deposition

Pollutants that have been moving through the atmosphere must finally settle somewhere on Earth. They may fall within a few yards or miles from their source, or many hundreds of miles away, across state and national borders. They may fall in dry particle or gaseous form. Or in any form of precipitation—rain, snow, sleet, hail, dew, clouds, or fog. Clouds in particular can be important sources of acid deposition, especially when they blanket forests for hours or days at a time. Generally, the areas with the most acid and toxic deposition are nearby or downwind from areas with the most emissions.

Scientists are working on ways to improve the measuring of acid deposition. Dry deposition is hard to measure, as is the acidity of clouds. Despite these difficulties, scientists have been able to come up with some reliable ways to measure acid deposition.

Deposition monitoring is performed by such government agencies as the EPA (Environmental Protection Agency) and NAPAP (National Acid Precipitation Assessment Program). The National Atmospheric Deposition Program monitors wet deposition in the United States at about 200 locations, every Tuesday morning all year long. Private organizations such as the National Audubon Society provide direction for monitoring by citizens and students.

Deposition collection equipment ranges from plastic buckets in which rain or snow is caught for analysis to more sophisticated instruments mounted on towers to monitor deposition from clouds. Monitoring is carried out in many places, including the mountains of New Hampshire, New York, and North Carolina.

On Mount Mitchell, North Carolina, scientists have measured the deposition of acids and ozone and studied their effects on trees. Two clear plastic chambers were constructed to create a greenhouse-like setting for the trees. One chamber received air filtered through carbon to remove impurities. The other received unfiltered (polluted) mountain air. In only six weeks, there was 50 percent less tree growth in the chamber with unfiltered mountain air.

Effects

Because so many factors are involved, the effects of acid rain—separate from other forms of air pollution—are difficult to pinpoint and prove. Some ecosystems can handle a high level of acidity while others can tolerate very little. The effects of acid and toxic rain are discussed in the next three chapters.

Two different kinds of acid rain monitoring stations: (left, a collecting station for both wet and dry deposition, and (below) a high tower that records air pollution from a nearby smokestack at various elevations.

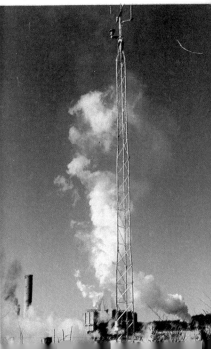

Chapter 5

Poisoned Lakes

 THE NORWEGIAN GOVERNMENT estimates that over half the fish in the lakes of southern Norway have died because of acidification. More than 18,000 lakes in Sweden have been acidified to the point where fish are endangered, if not eliminated. About 1,600 lakes in the province of Ontario alone, and 7,000 to 10,000 in all of eastern Canada are considered acidified. And many lakes in New England, Appalachia, and the upper Midwest are in danger of suffering the same fate.

All the plants and animals that live in and around a body of water are part of its *ecosystem*. Aquatic ecosystems include plants, many invertebrates, amphibians (frogs, toads, and salamanders), reptiles, birds, and mammals. Such ecosystems are delicately balanced, and even a small change can have a tremendous effect.

The introduction of acids into aquatic ecosystems that have little natural ability to neutralize them can cause serious trouble. Scientists have been studying the effects of acid rain on lakes and rivers for several decades.

How Acids Enter the Water

Acids and various other chemicals end up in lakes and streams in several ways. About half are deposited as dry particles in the air. The other half enter the water in wet form, which includes rain, snow, sleet, hail, dew, and fog.

Acids and toxic substances may also take a roundabout route into lakes and streams. For example, acid rain that falls on land may flow into sewage systems as runoff, or seep down into the underground water table, but it usually ends up in lakes or rivers. Acid rain runoff can wash many nutrients out of the soil and sometimes carries toxic metals

Spring acid shock, from the runoff of melting snow, may cause a sudden jolt in the acidity of a lake, even killing many fish (above). This scientist (right) is withdrawing snow from deep inside the winter snowpack to check it for pollutants that could cause acid shock if it melts rapidly in the spring.

released from the soil into lakes and rivers.

One of the most dangerous ways in which acids end up in lakes and rivers is known as *spring acid shock*. In the spring, if the snow melts rapidly, such as from a sudden temperature change, the acid and other pollutants that were deposited over winter are suddenly released into the soil. Then, carried by runoff, the acid enters lakes and rivers, streams and ponds. This large amount of acid can suddenly drop a pond's pH in just a couple of hours. The sudden change can be devastating to certain aquatic life forms. When additional acid enters the water with heavy spring rains, all the conditions are possible for disaster to occur in that body of water.

To make matters worse, the sudden springtime rise in acidity occurs when most aquatic life forms are highly vulnerable. Spring is the time when fish, amphibians, insects, and other arthropods reproduce. Eggs are laid in water and the young spend their early life there. They are in serious danger from sudden surges in acidity. Sometimes a whole generation of animal life in an aquatic ecosystem is wiped out by a particularly strong spring acid shock.

Neutralizing Capacity

Once acid arrives in a body of water, a number of factors determine just how much effect it will have. These factors include the water depth and surface area, its flushing capacity (the rate at which fresh water is added), and whether the body of water has contact with groundwater or receives its fresh water purely by rain and runoff. An additional factor—and probably the most important—is the neutralizing (sometimes called buffering) capacity of the watershed, which is the land from which water drains into a lake or river.

The following experiment will help you to understand how neutralizing works.

Cedar Pond, a lake in western Maine, is not now acidic, but it is vulnerable because the rock and soil surrounding it has little neutralizing capacity.

Neutralizing Acids with Bases

To perform this experiment, you will need at least one container (such as a small jar or test tube) of basic solution and one container of acidic solution. Make a good basic solution by putting one-fourth cup (60 milliliters) of distilled water in a container and mixing in one-half teaspoon of baking soda, crushed antacid tablets, or crushed blackboard chalk. For the acid solution, add about one tablespoon of vinegar or lemon juice to one-fourth cup (60 milliliters) of distilled water.

Test your basic solution with pH measuring

paper (see page 22) to make sure that it is indeed basic. Also test your acidic solution. Record their starting pH values.

Add several drops of basic solution to the acid. Gently swirl the container to mix. Now test the pH of this new solution. How has it changed? Continue adding basic solution, a small amount at a time, to the solution until it is neutral. You have buffered the acid to a neutral state. Record how much base it took to achieve this.

You can repeat this process using different combinations and strengths of acids and bases. Note which acids require more base added to become neutral and which bases buffer acids most quickly.

Different lakes have different neutralizing capacities, depending on the underlying and surrounding soil and rock in their watersheds. For example, limestone is a basic rock. Watersheds with a lot of limestone can neutralize acid rainfall fairly well, for a while anyway.

Granite, on the other hand, is a fairly acidic rock, with very little neutralizing capacity. Acid rain falling on a lake with granite surroundings stays acid and has a more profound effect. This is why acid rain tends to do so much damage in eastern Canada, where thin soils and granite bedrock have very limited neutralizing ability.

When rainfall with low pH continues to fall over a period of years, it wears away the neutralizing capacity of the area. Then, when acid rain continues to fall, the pH of the lake drops, and the lake becomes acidified. When the area's neutralizing ability is limited to begin with, damage can occur quickly.

The bedrock of the La Cloche Mountains in Ontario is the mineral quartzite, which is quite acidic. These lakes have little neutralizing capacity.

In just ten years, from 1961 to 1971, Lumsden Lake in the beautiful Killarney region of Ontario, Canada, went from a pH reading of 6.8 to 4.4. That's an increase in acidity of more than 200 times. Most lakes with dropping pH values are at higher elevations. These lakes are usually small and located in watersheds where the rock and soil have a low neutralizing capacity.

FACT

Even lakes located near each other can have very different neutralizing abilities because of their bedrock, and thus very different reactions to acid deposition. Three lakes in the Adirondacks within several miles of one another have very different pH values. All three receive acid rainfall of the same low pH level, but their neutralizing capacities are different. One lake has remained neutral, one is slightly acidic, and one is very acidic.

A relatively small percentage of the total number of lakes in the United States are considered completely acidified. However, the number of lakes located in areas of low neutralizing capacity is high. This means that more lakes could begin showing signs of acidification if acid rainfall continues.

Two lakes in a remote part of Maine near the Appalachian Trail are near each other geographically but are really very different. The one on the right is only slightly acidic (pH of 6.2) and has abundant fish and plant life. The one on the left has a pH of 5.1. It has very few trout still living in it.

As long as a lake's neutralizing capacity remains, it may appear to be healthy, even when it is on the brink of losing its fish population. The pH of the water may remain within the safe range, while the area's neutralizing capacity is gradually being worn away by continued acid deposition. Then, when the neutralizing capacity is exhausted, the pH of the water may suddenly drop.

All across the Northern Hemisphere, the natural neutralizers stored in our environment through the ages are being used up. Unless we make large cuts in fossil-fuel emissions, we may see increases in the number of acidified lakes and rivers in mountainous regions and in granite bedrock.

Neutralizing Capacities

An Earth Experience

To demonstrate how a body of water's neutralizing capacity can be used up, you will need three jars of water. Put some crushed chalk or other basic substance, such as antacid tablets, in one jar. Put just plain water in the second jar. Put a small amount of acid, such as a weak vinegar-water solution in the third jar.

Check the pH of the solution in each jar. The first should have a reading above 7, the second around 7, and the third one slightly below 7.

Now add a few drops of acid to each jar. Recheck the pH levels and record. Notice how the pH falls in the jars without neutralizing capacity (the ones without the base). Continue adding acid— a drop or so at a time—to jar number 1 until its pH drops below 6. This demonstrates how neutralizing capacity can be used up by continual acid deposition.

Life and Death in Lake 223

Scientists in Sweden and Norway were the first to make connections between acid rain and fish death. Later, experiments by Canadian and American scientists confirmed the earlier findings.

Some of these studies were done in natural settings. In the early 1970s, scientists selected a group of lakes in

A scientist gathers fish samples in a lake that is becoming acidified.

Ontario, Canada, for the study of pollution. Beginning in 1976, sulfuric acid was intentionally added to one of these lakes, which was called simply Lake 223. As the lake slowly acidified, scientists watched and carefully recorded the results.

During the first two years, the pH of Lake 223 was lowered from 6.8 to 5.8 and a number of changes in the food web were noted. Some species of small crustaceans died out and some fish began having trouble reproducing. By 1979, when the lake had reached a pH of 5.6, algae growth was affected, and several types of small fish, which were food sources for larger fish, died out.

Over the next year or two, some of the larger fish began having trouble reproducing. This meant that while there were still adult fish in the lake, fewer and fewer young fish were surviving. Scientists continued to record this steady decline during the following years. By 1983, when the acidity of Lake 223 had increased until its pH was 5, the few surviving fish were thin, distorted, and unable to reproduce. It was easy to see that the lake would soon have no fish.

What the Acid Does

Sulfuric acid in water affects fish in both direct and indirect ways. Directly, it affects their ability to take in oxygen, salt, and all the nutrients they need to stay alive.

Most lakes and streams normally have a pH between 6 and 8. At about pH 6, signs of damage start to appear. As the pH level of a lake drops below this point, one of the first effects might be a disruption of the food web as some of the most basic forms of food—the producers that feed the fish—start to die off. Mayflies and stoneflies, important food sources for fish, generally cannot survive when a lake's pH drops below 6. By the time pH drops to 5.5, many fish are unable to reproduce, and the young that hatch have difficulty staying alive. More and more adult fish become deformed and stunted due to lack of nutrients. If the pH continues to drop, the few remaining fish will probably die of suffocation. By the time the pH reaches 5, many kinds of fish disappear, and a lake with a pH below 4 has very different kinds of life in it if it has any at all.

Freshwater fish maintain a delicate balance of salts and minerals in their tissues through a process called osmoregulation. If the water that the fish take in through their gills contains acid, this process is upset. The acid molecules cause mucus to form on fish gills, making it harder for the fish to absorb oxygen. If enough mucus forms, the fish literally suffocate.

A pH that is too low also upsets the balance of salt in fish

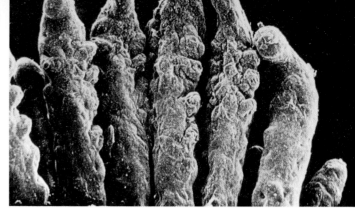

The gill arches of a fish, which are the organs where oxygen is taken from the water and carbon dioxide is given off, quickly show damage from metals in the water. The arches on the left are those of a healthy fish, greatly magnified. Those on the right have been damaged by aluminum.

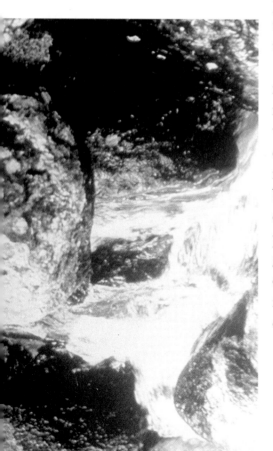

The water in this stream has been acidified, a condition that favors the growth of algae on the rocks.

tissue as well. Some fish have difficulty regulating their calcium needs. This means that fewer eggs are produced, and those that are formed are often too thin, too brittle, or otherwise damaged.

Calcium deficiency in fish can also cause deformed spines and other abnormalities. Crayfish tend to have this problem because they need calcium to replace their exterior skeleton (or exoskeleton) each time they molt.

Nitrogen in the water can have a very negative effect, particularly in areas where nitrogen-containing fertilizers are washed into waters from farmland runoff. The addition of even more nitrogen in acid rain causes too much algae to grow. That might seem to benefit the fish because they would have extra oxygen from the plants. But when so many plants die, the decomposition process uses a great deal of oxygen. As a result of these complex interactions, less oxygen is available for fish, further contributing to the breathing difficulties caused by acidic water.

Toxic Metals from the Soil

An indirect but equally deadly effect of acid rain is the release of heavy metals from the soil. These elements are harmless when they are bound up with other elements in the soil, but they can be harmful to living things when released.

Aluminum is one such mineral found in much of the Earth's surface. Generally it is part of harmless compounds, but acid rain causes the chemical bonds to be dissolved. Once released into soils and surface waters, aluminum can cause a great deal of harm. Among other effects, dissolved aluminum burns the gills of fish and accumulates in their organs, causing extensive damage.

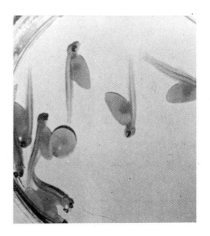

Aluminum poisoning can occur before damage from the acid itself occurs. For example, many fish can tolerate an acid level of pH 5.9. But a pH of 5.9 can release enough aluminum from surrounding soil to kill many fish. pH levels between 5.2 and 5.4 seem to be the range for greatest aluminum toxicity.

During spring acid shock, when the pH of lakes and streams can drop drastically in a matter

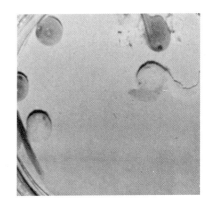

The larvae, or fry, of brown trout: In a lake with a fairly normal pH of 5.5 (top), the fry develop normally. When the pH has dropped to 5.0 (middle), the fry are somewhat damaged. The nutrients (yolk) from the original egg have not been absorbed by the developing young. If the pH drops even further, to 4.5 (bottom), the eggs fail to develop at all, and brown trout disappear from the lake.

of hours, the amount of aluminum in the water can rise just as dramatically. Some of this aluminum comes from runoff, having been released from nearby soils by acid rain. Some aluminum is released in the lake itself by its now acidic waters. Some aluminum that is a component of air pollution is deposited directly into the water by toxic rain.

Thus a great deal of aluminum can suddenly be found in a lake. Sometimes it is possible to see the silver sheen of that aluminum on the surface of a calm lake.

Unsafe to Eat. Not only are dissolved metals toxic to fish, but they are also dangerous for the larger animals (including humans) that eat the fish. Mercury, another metal that is released into water by acid rain and deposited by toxic rain, is also very dangerous to fish and to the people who eat fish. An amount of mercury as small as one tablespoon in a body of water that is 15 feet (4.6 meters) deep and the size of a football field is enough to make all the fish in that water unsafe to eat.

FACT

The "safe" level of mercury in food has been set at about 0.05 parts per million. Indians and Eskimos in parts of Canada and the United States eat fish and seal meat with mercury levels as high as 15.7 and even 37.2 parts per million.

The damage done by toxic metals is far-reaching. Some of these metals accumulate in the tissues of fish and, when the fish are eaten, they accumulate in the tissues of the people who eat the fish. The government of Ontario regularly pub-

Even when a lake does not appear to have been harmed, the fish in the lake may reveal acid damage. This scientist is using a net in a remote mountain lake to capture fish for testing.

lishes a list of lakes from which it is not safe to catch and eat the fish, particularly because of toxic metal content. This list includes most acidified lakes.

Humans and Frogs

Once a bountiful lake starts to acidify, sports and commercial fishermen must compete for those fish that remain. Disputes arise and neither group goes away satisfied. Sports fishermen lose their hobby and people who sell fishing supplies lose their income. Commercial fishermen find their whole way of life in jeopardy.

And it isn't just fish that are being harmed. All the plants, animals, and microscopic organisms that make up the aquatic ecosystem can be affected in some way. Bacteria that decompose leaves and other organic debris in surface water are weakened or killed. Some people refer to the fact that leaves can remain perfectly preserved in acid water for much longer than normal as the "pickling" effect.

Amphibians often disappear from acidified ecosystems. Frogs were here when the dinosaurs first appeared, and they survived when the dinosaurs became extinct. Now, all

Amphibians like this frog are particularly vulnerable to acid damage because they lay their eggs in the water of lakes and ponds. Many species of frogs are nearing extinction because their reproduction is interfered with by environmental pollution.

around the world, various species of frogs are suddenly becoming extinct. They are dying out because of pesticides, habitat destruction, global warming, and acid deposition in their habitats.

Amphibians cannot reproduce in an acidic environment. Acids make the membrane around amphibian embryos so tough that hatchlings are unable to break through at the proper time. Instead, they continue to grow, and when they finally do break out, they suffer from deformed spines. Then they are often killed by a fungus that acid has allowed to grow on their outer membranes.

Just as sad is the story of what acid rain does to birds and small mammals living on and near lakes and ponds. Like fish and amphibians, they suffer damage from the acid itself and indirect damage from metal poisoning and loss of food

supply. The osprey, loon, merganser, and kingfisher all eat fish. If they eat sick fish, they too become sick. If they breed, they produce thin-shelled eggs and deformed offspring. And when their food source dies out, these birds will die, too.

Studies have shown that thousands of lakes and rivers in the United States and Canada are showing—or are on the verge of showing—some effects of acid deposition. Many lakes and rivers are already dead—unable to support most life-forms. Others are dying a little each year—slowly, but very surely. The neutralizing capacities of tens of thousands of lakes are in danger of being used up. Those lakes will start to show damage soon unless something is done to reduce sulfur and nitrogen and other toxic emissions that start the damage in the first place.

Lakes of eastern North America are in danger from acid rain. The food web that supports large populations of ducks, such as the wood duck (below), *and other waterfowl can be disrupted. When fish are gone, much of the quiet sport* (above) *that people enjoy on lakes is also a thing of the past.*

Chapter 6

Forests and Farms

ACID RAIN FALLS not only on lakes, rivers, and streams, of course. But the link between acid rain and damage to land, or terrestrial, ecosystems is more complicated. It is harder to isolate a forest or a field and its life forms than it is to isolate an aquatic ecosystem. For one thing, many different types of plants and animals live on land. For another, land animals are more likely to come and go. Also, terrestrial ecosystems are more apt to change as a result of weather and other factors.

Timber growth has slowed at least 15 percent in Scandinavian countries in recent decades. In Germany, the problem is known as *Waldsterben,* which means "forest death". Scientists estimate that 50 percent or more of the great German forests are dead or dying.

Scientists, politicians, and industrialists disagree on just how much blame should be placed on acid rain over other factors in the environment for the deterioration of forests and croplands in industrial parts of the world. But the fact is that in many places forests and croplands *are* suffering. Few will deny that air pollution in general is probably a major factor, and many believe that acid deposition, which is just one form of the many kinds of air pollution, is involved in tree and plant death.

At the very least, acid deposition is a factor in forest stress. And trees under stress are more likely to suffer from adverse natural conditions than healthy trees are. The trees are damaged by the combined effects of sulfur dioxide, nitrogen oxides, ozone, and other gases, along with heavy metals and depleted soils. This combined attack leaves trees and other plants unable to cope with conditions that they might otherwise survive.

This dying red spruce forest in the central Adirondack Mountains is located at an elevation of 3,000 to 4,000 feet (925 to 1,230 meters), where it readily catches rain and winds filled with acid and other pollutants.

Soil and Acid Rain

Soil is made when rocks are broken down over long periods of time by wind and water and organic processes, such as the action of small animals and microscopic organisms. Soil may be acid, neutral, or basic, depending on the kind of rock it was made from.

Even soil made from acidic rock, such as granite, usually has enough neutralizing capacity to neutralize normal rain. But when very acidic rain falls over a short period of time, or slightly acidic rain falls frequently over a longer period, that neutralizing capacity can be wiped out. Then the soil itself becomes acidic. When acid rain falls on acid soil, the runoff that ends up in surface waters is likely to be very low in pH and very high in toxic metals.

As acid rain falls on leaves and needles of trees and other plants, it can directly damage these surfaces. In its gaseous form, sulfur dioxide can cause discoloration and leaching (washing out) of nutrients from leaves and needles.

When it falls on the ground, acid rain releases toxic minerals in the soil that can poison trees and plants. To make matters worse, acid rain can also wash away nutrients and kill helpful bacteria, fungi, and small mammals and invertebrates that are beneficial to soil and living systems. It can damage plant roots, making them less able to take in the needed nutrients.

To compensate for the acid in the environment, trees draw more basic compounds from the soil. Thus the soil's neutralizing capacity is being used up just when the need for neutralizing increases. As a result of this, trees and plants become weakened. They grow more slowly and are less able to resist disease, harmful insects, and bad weather.

The situation is hard to evaluate because much of the damage to land systems is hidden—it is often not obvious that tree growth has slowed. By the time forests start showing symptoms of damage, the

An instrument called a lysimeter is used to collect moisture in soil in order to measure the way acid rain and other liquids percolate through the ground.

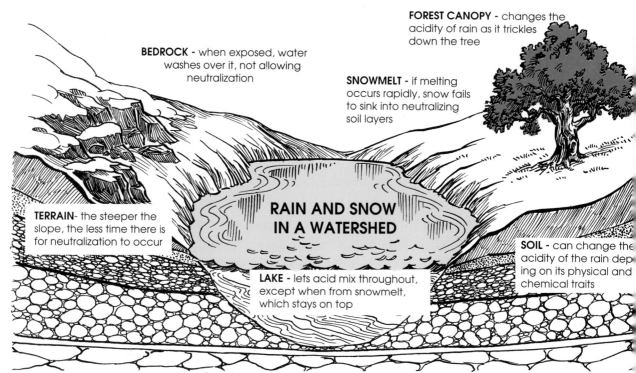

FOREST CANOPY - changes the acidity of rain as it trickles down the tree

BEDROCK - when exposed, water washes over it, not allowing neutralization

SNOWMELT - if melting occurs rapidly, snow fails to sink into neutralizing soil layers

RAIN AND SNOW IN A WATERSHED

TERRAIN - the steeper the slope, the less time there is for neutralization to occur

SOIL - can change the acidity of the rain dep ing on its physical and chemical traits

LAKE - lets acid mix throughout, except when from snowmelt, which stays on top

Even after rain falls, its effect on the land and a lake can be changed by the structure of the land and the things growing on it.

reaction has been going on for a long time. And even when the damage becomes obvious—such as when leaves shrivel up and fall off in June—it is difficult to point a finger at one factor and say that it was the cause.

For these reasons, millions of dollars have been spent in the past decade to study the effects of acid rain on the land and on the things that grow on it. And much has been learned.

Scientists have found that all the components in acid deposition—sulfur and nitrogen particles, sulfur dioxide and nitrogen oxide gases, sulfuric and nitric acid, and secondary pollutants such as ozone—can be harmful to plants and soil. Mountainside forests located at high elevations are frequently bathed in highly polluted, misty air. They may be especially vulnerable. But almost any area downwind of fossil-fuel burning is exposed to enough acid to be harmed.

Measuring Soil pH

Plants need a healthy environment just as humans do. But plants can't run away from an unhealthy place nor can they select clean food. Most plants grow best in soil that is neutral or slightly basic. However, some plants, such as oak trees and mosses, thrive in soil that is somewhat acidic.

In this experiment you will test the pH of a variety of soils. Collect a number of soil samples from different types of locations. Using a small shovel—not your hands—scoop a small amount into a piece of newspaper, fold it up, and record the site. Try to get a soil sample from the ground near a factory that is sending smoke into the air. Collect soil near a busy highway where automobiles and trucks are spewing out emissions. If possible, get some soil from a farm; some from beneath coniferous trees (cone-bearing, such as firs and pines); and some from beneath deciduous trees (hardwoods, such as maples and oaks). You might also want to test soil from your own backyard.

Before you run the pH test, be sure that the soil is dry. Do not touch it with your hands—they may contaminate your sample. You can buy a soil-test kit at a nursery or hardware store. The directions are in the kit. Test each soil sample. Record the pH for each.

Once you know the pH of the soil from the various sites, you might want to try growing something in your samples. Place some of each sample in a small container, making sure to label it. Then plant a couple of seeds in each. Which kind of soil seems best for your seeds to grow in?

Acid Rain and the Timber Industry

The timber industry is one of the giant businesses of the world. When forests are damaged by air pollutants, the supplies of wood cut by timber companies can shrink.

Much of the damage to forests seems to occur when elevated levels of both sulfur dioxide and ozone are found together. The Environmental Protection Agency (EPA), which sets standards for ozone levels, has determined that a concentration of 120 parts per billion should not be reached more than once per year—and then only for a matter of minutes. During the summer of 1986, that level was exceeded *eleven times* on the slopes of Mount Mitchell, North Carolina, the highest peak on the East Coast. And the high levels lasted for several hours each time. The pH readings of clouds that settled over the mountaintop ranged between 2.4 and 4.7. Plant scientist Robert I. Bruck has watched the decline of what was once a thriving forest ecosystem along the ridge of the Appalachian Mountains. He says it is difficult to prove that air pollution is the cause, but he knows that the forests are dying.

Conifers such as fir, spruce, and pine are especially threatened, but such hardwood species as beech and oak are also affected. Millions of acres of trees across much of Europe, especially in England, Scandinavia, Germany, Poland, and Czechoslovakia, are dying. Some North American forests, especially in the Adirondacks, and the remainder of the Appalachian mountain region, as well as in Ontario and Quebec in Canada, also seem to be declining.

The timber industry is very important in many areas of North America and Europe. In Europe, forests are currently being overcut to eliminate dying trees. Even if damage ceased immediately—which is virtually impossible—this overcutting will still result in future shortages of timber and financial losses to the industry.

Forestry is an industry worth $10 billion a year in Canada. About 10 percent of all Canadian jobs depend on the harvesting and processing of trees. When forests are in danger, those jobs may disappear, too.

FACT

Besides supplying timber for wood and wood by-products, trees are important for many reasons. Trees are a vital part of the Earth's evaporation-transpiration water cycle. They hold soil in place with their roots. They nourish the soil when leaves and dead branches are allowed to decompose, thus playing a part in the oxygen-carbon dioxide balance and helping to prevent global warming. And trees provide a habitat for wildlife. These factors are reasons for making sure that forests are protected.

Forests may die when they are attacked by air pollution. Acid rain appears to affect the trees in at least two different ways: first, the leaves are damaged by direct contact with acid precipitation and they soon fall off (left), *so that the tree can no longer make its own food by photosynthesis; and second, the acid in the soil* (above) *releases metals, which are then free to harm the forest even further.*

How Plants Are Damaged

Conifers are among the trees most damaged by pollutants, including ozone. Damage is generally first seen at the top, or crown, of the tree, and at the tips of lower branches. Needles on conifers turn brown and fall off, leaving bare branches that make "evergreen" seem like the wrong name. When a tree is near death, it may produce a large quantity of cones as it tries to reproduce itself before dying.

Some deciduous trees are also being damaged. In parts of Canada, the maple syrup industry is in crisis because of extensive damage to sugar maple groves. Because of acid deposition and the toxic metals that acid releases in the soil, the maples seem to have a hard time taking in the water they need. After a while trees look as if they were suffering the effects of drought, even when there has been plenty of rain.

The leaves turn brown and fall off in August, and in spring, the trees don't produce the sap from which syrup is made.

Metals. As acid rain falls from the needles and leaves of trees to the forest floor, additional damage may occur. The acid works its way into the ground and a number of things begin to happen. One of the first effects is the release of toxic metals.

We've already discussed the negative effects that aluminum can have in aquatic ecosystems. It is no more friendly to terrestrial ecosystems. It affects the fine roots of trees and is drawn up into the very fiber of the tree itself. Once inside the tree, the metal makes it more and more difficult for the tree to live. It also weakens the tree's long roots, making it more likely that strong winds will knock it down.

Other toxic metals, such as lead and mercury, whether deposited on forest soil from toxic rain or released by acid rain, can cause similar problems.

Toxic metals can also be harmful to animals. These metals can settle in grassy fields where livestock graze or in the water they drink. When the animals ingest them, these toxic metals will accumulate in the organs and fatty tissues. This accumulation is good neither for the animals themselves nor for the human beings who eat them.

And wild animals are in just

Botanists with the federal government are continually studying how plants and soil are affected by acid rain.

as much danger. A poisoned food and water supply is a serious danger to all animals, from waterfowl such as ducks and geese to such woodland creatures as raccoons and moose. It is also a danger to the animals (and humans) who consume them. Higher than normal amounts of mercury, cadmium, and other toxic metals have been found in the tissues and organs of many wild animals in areas where the soil and water are acidic.

Nutrient Loss. While these toxic metals are being deposited, important nutrients are being washed away. Acid rain can leach nutrients out of leaves. On the forest floor, an acid environment changes the chemistry of nutrients and roots, making nutrients unavailable and roots unable to receive them. Just as osmoregulation in fish keeps their various nutrient needs in balance, trees have systems that control the absorption and release of the substances they need. An acidic environment can upset this balance and harm the tree.

For example, all plants must have calcium, potassium, and magnesium to survive. Calcium is used in building cell walls. Potassium helps plants fight disease and strengthens them. Magnesium is a necessary element in the production of chlorophyll. But acid rain disrupts these processes and washes these nutrients out of the soil.

The roots of plants take in these nutrients in exchange for excess hydrogen, which they release into the soil. When soil is acidic, however, there is already an excess of hydrogen in the soil, and this complex process breaks down, leaving the plant unable to take in nourishment.

A malnourished plant or tree is more likely to be hurt by disease and other stresses. Just as you function better and

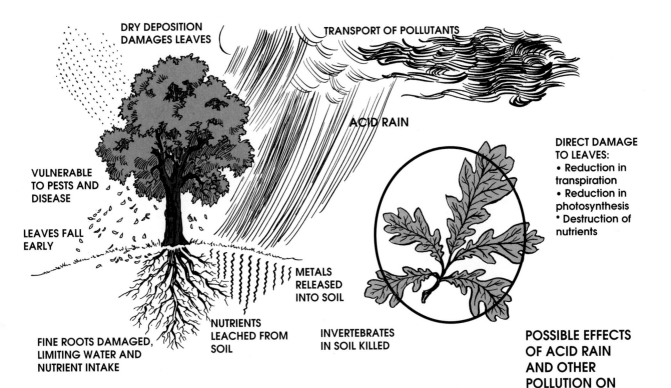

DRY DEPOSITION DAMAGES LEAVES

TRANSPORT OF POLLUTANTS

ACID RAIN

VULNERABLE TO PESTS AND DISEASE

LEAVES FALL EARLY

FINE ROOTS DAMAGED, LIMITING WATER AND NUTRIENT INTAKE

NUTRIENTS LEACHED FROM SOIL

METALS RELEASED INTO SOIL

INVERTEBRATES IN SOIL KILLED

DIRECT DAMAGE TO LEAVES:
• Reduction in transpiration
• Reduction in photosynthesis
• Destruction of nutrients

POSSIBLE EFFECTS OF ACID RAIN AND OTHER POLLUTION ON FORESTS

stay healthier when you eat properly, so do well-nourished trees. Although not eating right won't actually give you a cold, it will make your body less able to resist one if you are exposed. In the same way, trees stressed by acid rain are less able to handle normal environmental stresses.

Some people claim that acid rain doesn't kill trees. Technically, they might be right. But acid rain helps create an environment in which some species of trees cannot live. Many other people say that's the same thing as killing trees. What do you think?

Besides releasing toxic metals and leaching away nutrients, acid rain also affects organisms living in the soil. Many beneficial bacteria, such as the bacteria that make nitrogen in the soil available to plants, may be killed by an acid environment. The bacteria that help to decompose organic matter such as fallen leaves and dead plants are also slowed down or killed. As a result, the beneficial nutrients stored in decomposing plants and animals are not made available to living plants. As beneficial bacteria die out, disease-causing fungi take hold, afflicting plants with stem and root rot.

The burrowing of earthworms through soil makes oxygen available to plant roots and provides better soil drainage. Some studies indicate that earthworms may not survive in acidic soil. The lack of earthworms in forest soil—or any other kind of soil, for that matter—means that the entire ecosystem is unhealthy.

An Earth Experience

How Acid Rain Gets into Plants

Acid rain and dry pollutants shower down on plants, settling on leaves and young growing stems. Most of these chemicals are not absorbed through the tough epidermis or bark of the plant. Instead they fall to the ground and are taken up by the root system and get inside the plant.

Select corn, bean, or radish seeds for this experiment. Fill three

pots with good, rich soil. Be sure the pots have a hole in the bottom and a saucer to catch the excess water. Plant five seeds in each pot at the same depth. Keep the pots watered until the seedlings are several inches tall.

You are now ready to start the experiment. You will be using a red-colored vinegar solution to represent acid rain—just add a teaspoon of vinegar to a cup of water. Put a few drops of red vegetable dye in this solution so that you can detect its pathway through the plant.

In pot number 1, pour the acid rain solution directly on the soil. In pot number 2, spray the acid rain solution with a spray bottle or atomizer on the plant parts above the soil. While doing this, cover the soil with aluminum foil so that only the leaves get the acid. Water the soil of this plant with tap water, which simulates clean rain (unless, of course, your tap water is acidic, in which case you will need to use bottled water—test it to be sure). Pot number 3 is your control. It receives only clean water.

After a period of several weeks, measure the height of the plants in all three pots. Cut off a plant in pot number 1 and examine the tissue inside the stem. Note the small red spots. These are the conducting tubes or vascular vessels that carry the water and pollutants in the soil to all parts of the plant.

Do you detect any differences in size, strength, and color in the plants? Can you draw conclusions about the effect of the acidic solution on growing plants?

The radishes on the left were subjected to the most acid rain. Did you get similar results?

77

Wheat is one of the most important crops in the United States and Canada. But where the soil is shallow, as it is in eastern Canada, cropland is vulnerable to acid rain.

Cropland

Of course, rain does not fall only on forests. It falls just as often on the land that produces the crops we eat. If acid deposition has negative effects on soil, it is easy to see that the things we grow in soil are also at risk.

Many crops, including grains, such as wheat, barley, and alfalfa, and vegetables, such as peas, carrots, lettuce, beans, and broccoli, are sensitive to ozone and other air pollution damage. Acid causes some leafy plants to retain abnormally large amounts of toxic substances. For example, lettuce leaves grown in an acidic environment will retain more cadmium—a toxin—than they would otherwise. Soybeans, a vital cash crop in the United States, are harmed by pollution.

About 50 percent of Canada's best farmland is in areas that are most heavily hit with acid rain, which originates primarily in the factories and power plants of the United States. This is the part of Canada that has thin soil over acidic bedrock.

In areas of low pH rainfall, farmers often add lime to the soil to counteract acidity. Fertilizers are also used to replace some of the nutrients leached away by acid rain. But overuse of fertilizers creates its own problems. In addition, fertilizers are very expensive to use regularly, increasing the cost of our food supplies. Lime and fertilizers do nothing to correct the damage done by toxic metals that fall in the rain or are released from the soil by acid rain.

More than 600,000 tons (540,000 metric tons) of lime are applied each year to Swedish farm fields to neutralize acidity. Such liming of fields resolves the immediate problem of soil acidity but does nothing to solve the acid rain crisis.

FACT

To sum up, what does acid rain damage mean to terrestrial ecosystems? It means that trees grow more slowly and produce less wood. This fact of acid rain has already hurt the lumber, pulp, and paper industries, especially in Canada.

It means lower production and higher costs for raising crops, which affects farm income and the cost of our food. It means increased danger of contaminated food for all of us.

It means that increasing numbers of wildlife species will become endangered as their food sources are poisoned. Many are already in danger because of other environmental problems.

It means that the beauty of unspoiled forests may slowly give way to dead and dying trees where nothing can live and people can find no pleasure.

Can you put a price tag on all of that damage?

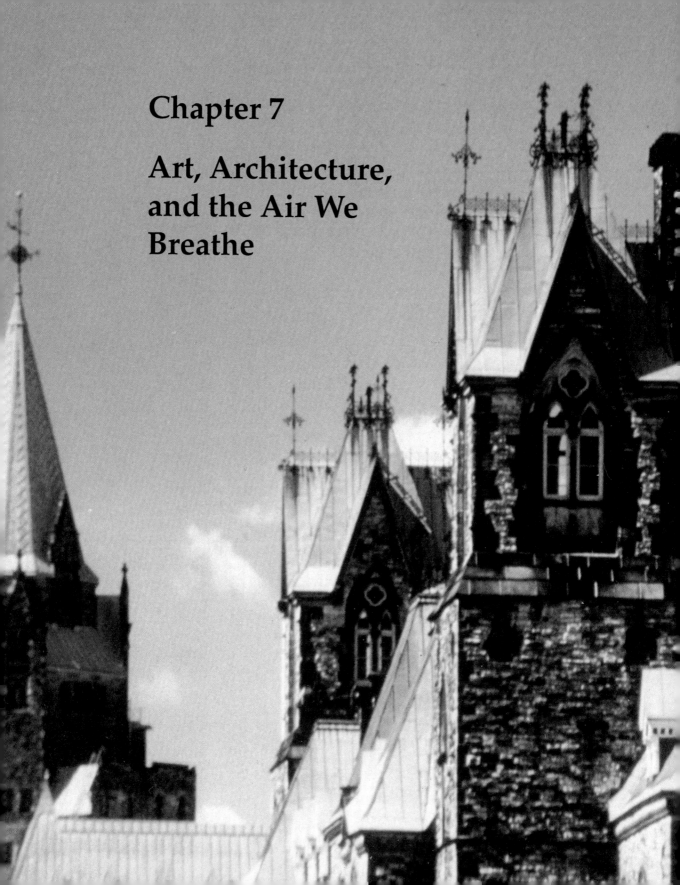

Chapter 7

Art, Architecture, and the Air We Breathe

WE'VE DISCUSSED how sulfur and nitrogen emissions mix with oxygen and water to become acid rain. We've looked at the effects of acid rain on aquatic and terrestrial ecosystems.

But acid deposition damages other things too. The dry particles of sulfur and nitrogen compounds circulate in the air with dust. They are deposited on buildings and statues and automobiles, and they are breathed into the lungs of human beings.

Acid Pollution and Haze

Dry particles of many pollutants enter the atmosphere and attach themselves to the dust and dirt that drifts in the air. If you've ever looked at a shaft of sunlight, you've seen tiny dust particles dancing in midair. When there are lots of such particles in the air, they scatter light, which results in poor visibility. That means that you can no longer see long distances through so much pollution. Among the pollutants that contribute to haze in the air are sulfates, nitrates, hydrocarbons, and ozone.

Today, the visibility in most areas of the eastern United States is generally under 15 miles (24 kilometers), down from a seemingly endless 40 to 70 miles (64 to 108 kilometers) over the last 40 years.

Haze doesn't seem very important at first, but it can have serious economic effects. Decreased visibility means loss of income in tourist areas. Who will climb to a scenic viewpoint when acid haze hides the scenery?

Unseen National Parks. In the 50 national parks where air pollution is regularly measured, pollution has affected visibility more than 90 percent of the time. Tourists who flock to the Grand Canyon, often from as far away as Europe, Asia, and Australia, sometimes find air pollution so thick that not even the opposite rim of the canyon can be seen, let alone the Colorado River below.

The single largest source of sulfur emissions in the West is the coal-burning power plant at Page, Arizona, about 80 miles (128 kilometers) from the Grand Canyon. The plant burns a low-sulfur coal but uses special machinery to lessen the sulfur content of its emissions. The plant's owners argue that we can't be sure that its emissions are responsible for poor visibility and sulfur dioxide deposition in the Grand Canyon. But the 200 tons (180 metric tons) of sulfur dioxide that the plant spews out into the air each day while operating at full capacity aren't doing anyone or anything any good.

Airplanes and the Arctic. Acid haze also makes aircraft navigation difficult and dangerous. Even the Alaskan Arctic, where you would expect the air to be very clear, is threatened. Since World War II, pilots flying over this area during late winter and early spring, have noticed hazy skies that looked more like Los Angeles smog than the northern lights. This haze is caused by pollution coming from industrial parts of the world, particularly Eastern Europe and the Soviet Union.

Just as acid haze interferes with our ability to view things at a distance, it also interferes with the flow of light and warmth from the sun to the Earth and back into the atmosphere. This kind of interference is occurring in the Arctic.

Arctic ecosystems are *very* delicately balanced. Some-

Beautiful vistas across the Grand Canyon (above) *have fallen victim to acid haze, which forms in the canyon region, perhaps from smoke given off by the huge power plant 80 miles (128 kilometers) away (see page 15). It is now difficult to see across to the far rim (below).*

thing that endangers even one species can have a harmful effect on the whole system. For example, acid rain seems to hamper the growth of lichen, a small plant that is a combination of algae and fungi. Lichen is an important source of food for caribou, or reindeer. If lack of lichen makes it difficult for caribou to live, it also affects animals such as the bear and the wolf, which feed on caribou.

Damage to Structures

Loss of visibility is one of the costs of acid deposition that is hard to measure. Damage to buildings, cars, and other man-made items is much easier to measure and to put a price tag on. The cost of damage to buildings, monuments, and other such structures in Europe is estimated at about $20 billion per year. For the United States, the cost is about $5 billion.

Treasures of History. Gravestones on the Gettysburg Battlefield and in cemeteries across the country are being eaten away. If you take a walk through an old cemetery, you will probably find it difficult to read the inscriptions and dates on the stones because weather and pollution have blurred the letters.

Damage is done to human structures that are continually exposed to acid rain and other air pollution. For example, acid rain speeded up the normal deterioration of a stucco wall by changing the chemistry of the material.

An ancient cemetery in Krakow, Poland, has been almost destroyed by the pollutants from nearby factories.

The Effect of Acid Rain on Building Materials

Collect several materials used in the construction of buildings, monuments, tombstones, bridges, fences, and other objects that are constantly exposed to the weather. These might include small pieces of limestone, marble, sandstone, brick, concrete, raw wood, painted wood, aluminum, steel, or copper. You will need two samples of each material, one to be used for the experiment and one for a control.

In the real world, the effect of acid rain on many of these materials would take months or years to detect. To speed up the process for purposes of this experiment, you will have to apply an acidic solution daily for a number of weeks, or until you notice a change in the material.

Place one each of the samples of building material on each of two pans or cookie sheets. Using a spray bottle, apply a vinegar solution (about half a cup of water to one tablespoon of vinegar) to the objects in one pan. This is simulating acid rain. Use another spray bottle filled with tap or bottled water to spray clean rain on the second pan, which is your control. Spray the samples each day and dump out the extra water as it accumulates.

As soon as you notice any change in color or disintegration of a material, record your observations. Which materials were damaged the most or the quickest? You might try the same experiment placing the materials outdoors in the sun and wind. How are the results different?

Take a ride around the countryside to examine the materials used in old houses and in houses recently built. Which materials seem to hold up best under damaging weather conditions?

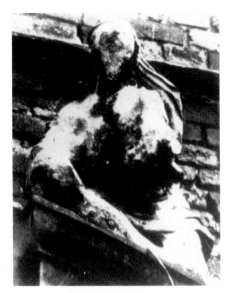

This statue was erected on a castle in Germany in 1702. Two hundred years later, the photo on the left was taken. The statue showed little real damage in 200 years. The photo on the right, however, was taken in 1969, only 67 years later. The figure's features are completely eroded by air pollution.

The Taj Mahal is an incredibly beautiful building erected by an emperor in India in memory of his wife. This 350-year-old marble-and-sandstone structure is being threatened by acid rain and other air pollution.

The Parthenon, a temple to the goddess Athena, is crumbling, having suffered more damage from air pollution in the last several decades than in all the twenty-five hundred years since it was built on the highest hill in Athens, Greece.

There are two Cleopatra's Needles, tall columns built in Egypt three thousand years ago. One was taken to London, England, about a hundred years ago. The other was placed in New York City's Central Park. They have both suffered more damage from heavily sulfur-laden air in the past one hundred years than in the previous three thousand years of their existence. The ornate carvings that told tales of ancient Egypt are now unreadable.

The Capitol buildings in Washington, D.C., and in Ottawa, Canada (see page 80), are also disintegrating from air pollution. Part of the Jefferson Memorial has been shut down because it is crumbling. Limestone and marble turn to gypsum in the presence of excessive amounts of sulfur dioxide. Gypsum is a crumbly substance that washes away in the rain.

In 1984 millions of dollars were spent to restore the Statue of Liberty, which had been severely corroded by air pollutants. The combination of sulfur dioxide and high humidity speeds up the corrosion of metals so that sometimes rust can almost form literally right before your eyes. B-52 bombers and other U.S. weapons systems have corrosion problems that are aggravated by acid rain.

The Effect of Acid Rain on Fabrics

An Earth Experience

You will need two pieces each of nylon, cotton, silk, or other fabrics for this experiment. One piece of each will be used for testing and the second one for the control. Construct a number of small wooden frames on which the material may be stretched and tacked in place. Fill one spray bottle with bottled water to represent clean rain, and another with a solution of half a cup of water to one teaspoon of vinegar to be the acid rain.

Spray the acid solution on each test fabric every day. Spray the second piece of each fabric with clean water. Be sure the fabrics dry out between "rains." Do this for a period of several weeks. Examine the material closely. Is there any evidence of breaking or disintegrating threads? Are you able to tear the test fabric more easily than the control? What has happened to the color? Record your findings.

Damage to Fabrics

Stone and steel are not the only materials being damaged by air pollution. Flags that fly from public buildings in large cities fade and wear out faster than flags in small towns and rural areas, thanks to acids and other pollutants.

The cloth, leather, and fine paper of books and other items in museums and libraries are also being damaged by ozone, even though they are not outdoors. Sulfur particles enter libraries and museums through ventilation systems and destroy works of culture and art centuries old. Some museums and libraries have installed special ventilation systems to prevent pollutants in the outside air from ruining their treasures.

Damage to Humans

On top of the billions of dollars of damage done to physical structures is the cost of health damage to human beings. Health-care costs stemming from sulfur compounds in the air are estimated at about $2 billion annually.

Researchers have found a direct association between air-pollution levels and deaths related to lung and heart disease. Since many North Americans live in the areas of highest air-pollution concentration—around the Great Lakes and Ohio River Valley and along the East Coast—many people are placed at high risk of suffering and even dying from pollution-related causes. In Canada, 80 percent of the people live in the most polluted areas.

The U.S. Congress Office of Technology Assessment estimates that about 50,000 Americans and Canadians die each year from illnesses caused by sulfur pollution. The figure would be much higher if we included deaths related to nitrogen oxide emissions, ozone, and poisoning by toxic metals released into the environment by acid rain. And some scientists suspect that acid rain plays a part in the increasing number of deaths from various forms of cancer.

And that's just the people that actually die. Hundreds of thousands more suffer from lung and heart disease, as well as respiratory infections due to lung irritation.

Breathing Problems. When sulfur dioxide levels in the air increase, so do coughs, sore throats, bronchitis, and lung disease. Even at levels that meet EPA standards, tiny sulfate particles can be drawn deep into highly sensitive areas of the lungs. Within minutes of exposure to sulfur emissions, asthma sufferers can experience difficulty breathing. If you've ever watched a person struggle for a breath of air, you know how scary this can be. How can we justify continuing to create conditions that make it difficult for people to *breathe?*

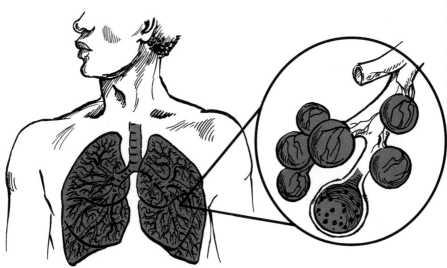

Sulfur dioxide particles in the air are inhaled into the lungs, where they spread out evenly on every surface, even into the tiny alveoli, where oxygen exchange takes place.

FACT

In August 1987, over one hundred people were treated for eye, throat, and mouth irritation when 2 tons (1.8 metric tons) of highly toxic sulfur trioxide gas leaked from an Inco plant near Sudbury, Ontario. Even without accidents, the sulfur dioxide regularly emitted from Inco smokestacks has been linked to chronic bronchitis in Inco employees.

We know that continued exposure to even low levels of sulfur dioxide hurts human lungs. We know that children who are regularly exposed to sulfur dioxide are likely to have more frequent and more severe respiratory infections than other children. It appears that the same is true for nitrogen oxide emissions. The American Lung Association and other organizations studying pollution-related illnesses believe that unless sulfur dioxide emissions are severely cut back in the near future, the health of the general public will decline.

Again, this is a problem of global proportions. In parts of Europe it is much worse than in North America. In the late 1980s, Hungarian experts estimated that the five-year cost to their economy due to air pollution-related illnesses and premature death was $374 million. In Hungary the heaviest concentration of sulfates and other airborne pollutants is found in two "pollution corridors" where 40 percent of the population lives.

Metals in the Environment

In Krakow, Poland, the air is heavy with dirt and dust as well as other pollutants such as heavy metals and gases from

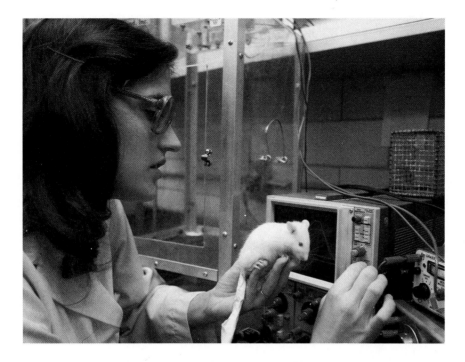

Scientists study the lungs of rats that have been exposed for long periods to air pollution. These test animals have a higher occurrence of cancer and other serious diseases than rats not exposed to the pollutants.

mining and industry. Breathing this polluted air is taking a terrible toll. In Katowice, near the Silesian Industrial Zone, there is more cancer, respiratory infection, and circulatory illness than anywhere else in Poland. Krakow has the highest infant mortality rate. The quantity of toxic metals in the environment, especially lead, is being blamed for increases in the number of mentally handicapped children.

The air in this area is so heavily polluted with dirt, dust, and other contaminants that when it rains people call it "mud rain." Lead literally rains down from the smokestacks of local industry. Mud rain is deposited in gardens, where it is absorbed by plants. Children, and adults as well, eat fruit and vegetables laced with lead, cadmium, copper, and zinc. These metals have been linked to brain damage, kidney, liver, and circulatory disorders, cancer, and anemia.

When the Communist
governments of Poland
and East Germany fell
in 1989 and 1990, the
Western world became
more aware of the toxic-
metal-laden "mud rain"
that had long been
damaging the environ-
ment and the health of
people who lived near
the factories.

One of the toxic metals released into the environment by
acid rain is mercury, which is dissolved in the presence of
acid. In the soil it is absorbed by plants, which are then eaten
by animals. Even if it doesn't hurt the animal right away, it
accumulates in its tissues. If that animal is eaten by humans,
it can have serious effects.

Even very small amounts of mercury can cause brain
damage in unborn children. Accumulated mercury in the
tissue of all humans can lead to nerve disorders, brain damage, and death. Many lakes that have low pH have high
levels of mercury, which means that fish in those lakes are
likely to be contaminated with mercury. Physicians routinely

warn pregnant women to avoid eating certain kinds of fish because of the danger of mercury poisoning.

Aluminum is also found in our surface and ground waters. Aluminum seems to have played a part in the deaths of several kidney patients who were on dialysis, a medical process by which the kidneys are cleaned artificially. Aluminum is also suspected of playing a part in Alzheimer's disease, a brain disorder.

Even the pipes that carry drinking water into our houses can be the source of problems. In Boston, for example, reservoirs are becoming increasingly acidic. As the water moves through pipes made of such metals as copper and lead, particles of the metal can be leached from the pipes into the water we drink.

In a coal-mining region of Pennsylvania, ground and surface waters were so badly polluted by mining operations that many people have turned to the sky for their water. As in olden days and other parts of the world, they installed cisterns to capture rainfall. But then it was discovered that the rain was contaminated with acid that leached dangerous levels of copper and lead from the cisterns. The people had to have water shipped in from other places.

Between the toxins that fall from the sky in acid and toxic rain and the toxins that are released in soil and water by acid rain, twentieth-century humans have inadvertently been conducting chemistry experiments on their own bodies. We are continually exposing ourselves to greater amounts of dangerous substances as the price we pay for being dependent on fossil fuels.

In some way, we all pay the price.

Chapter 8

**Priority One:
Reduce Emissions**

THE GOOD NEWS about acid rain is that we know exactly what causes it—the emissions that come from the burning of fossil fuels. We know that if we reduce emissions, we will reduce acid rain and the damage it causes. But different groups of citizens often have different ideas on how this should be done.

First we will discuss what can be done to reduce the emissions. Then we will discuss ways of getting these things done. Finally, we will discuss what *you* can do to take action against acid rain.

Liming

Liming is the process of adding lime, an alkaline substance, to water or soil that has been acidified. The lime acts as a neutralizing agent, and usually succeeds in bringing the pH of the water or soil closer to neutral.

Liming is not really a solution, it is a treatment. Just as cough medicine quiets a cough but doesn't cure the underlying illness, liming deals with the effects of acid deposition but doesn't solve the problem.

The addition of lime does nothing to eliminate the cause of the acidity, which is the sulfur and nitrogen emissions, probably from faraway locations. So in order to keep the pH level up, the process has to be repeated again and again—an expensive procedure.

Also, liming does nothing to reduce the toxic metals that have been released into the water or soil. Even if you restore the pH level of a lake, fish may still die of aluminum poisoning. You can add lime to a field of crops, but if it is continually rained on by water polluted with lead or other metals, the crops will still be contaminated. And liming doesn't

work at all for forests because it is difficult to apply the lime. If you dump it from a plane, you merely cover the canopy of treetops. If you truck it into the forest, people have to be paid to spread it on the forest floor.

In some instances, liming is an expensive but somewhat effective short-term treatment. But that is all.

Conservation

The number one answer to reducing sulfur dioxide and nitrogen oxide emissions is energy conservation. Even when energy does not cost much at the cash register, we must consider its cost to the environment.

This is a cost that you will have to pay as adults and that your children will have to pay when they become adults. Less energy used means less fossil fuel burned, so when we conserve energy we conserve valuable natural resources. And as an added bonus, reducing emissions by energy conservation saves money!

Alternate Energy Sources

In the 1970s, an oil crisis was created when the oil-producing nations got together and agreed to limit their production and raise their prices. At that time, there was a lot of talk about finding alternate energy sources, so that we wouldn't have to depend on foreign oil. However, when the price of oil went down, people went back to burning coal and oil without thinking. But the oil won't last forever.

The use of windmills to turn wind energy into electricity is one way of limiting the acid rain that damages the environment.

The war in the Persian Gulf in 1991 reminded us that our dependence on fossil fuels makes us vulnerable to political situations and continues to harm the environment. We must start developing new ways to harness energy sources that will not harm the environment. The possibilities are really quite exciting.

Wind. For centuries humans have used windmills to harness the wind for energy. Once they were used to grind wheat and corn into flour, but more recently windmills have been used to turn the turbines that create electricity.

Hydroelectric, or water, power (above) *and solar energy, such as that being used to run experimental cars* (above right), *make electricity without burning fossil fuels that harm the environment.*

Water. Water can be a very powerful, very clean source of energy. Large electricity-generating dams such as Hoover Dam and Glen Canyon Dam supply thousands of megawatts of power to many large cities.

These huge dams are not without their environmental costs, however. Some experts think that it would be better to have many smaller dams to provide electricity for towns and cities—and even individual households in rural areas.

Sun. Solar energy is limitless, it is clean, and we don't have to buy it from another country. The sun can be used directly to heat homes or indirectly by using the heat to produce electricity to run machinery. Solar rays can also be converted into electricity with solar cells and arrays.

Geothermal energy. *Geothermal* means "Earth heat." The inside of the Earth is very hot, and sometimes that heat escapes through natural vents such as geysers. That heat can be put to work heating buildings or generating electricity. Other geothermal sources include hot-water reservoirs in Texas and Louisiana and hot springs. In addition, there are collections of hot, dry rock underground in some places through which water pipes could be passed for heating.

Although geothermal energy is being used in a variety of places around the world to generate electricity, this energy source has not yet been fully developed. The energy source is free, but the utilization of it is not.

In Reykjavik, the capital of Iceland, a system of pipes delivers hot water from hot springs to 90 percent of the homes. There are about 250 other locations on the frigid island of Iceland where hot springs occur and could be used.

FACT

We Still Need to Use Coal

Despite all the coal that has been used since the beginning of the Industrial Revolution, there are still massive quantities below the surface of the Earth. While we are not going to eliminate it as an energy source, there are things we can do to lessen the impact of coal burning on the environment.

Low-Sulfur Fuels. One way to reduce sulfur emissions is by coal switching—switching from high-sulfur coal to low-sulfur coal.

Much of the coal mined in the eastern part of the United States is bituminous, sometimes called soft coal, which is high in sulfur content. However, it is also high in heat value—the amount of heat it produces—when burned. Much of the coal in the western part of the United States is lignite. Lignite is lower in sulfur content, but it is also lower in heat value, which makes it a less efficient form of fuel. (Anthracite, or hard coal, is the best. It has a low sulfur content and gives off high heat.)

Since most of the industry in the United States is in the northeast and north-central states, it is more convenient to use high-sulfur eastern coal. Some users have switched to low-sulfur western coal, but their fuel costs more because of the price of transportation.

There is the added problem that if a lot of industries switch coal, areas where bituminous coal is mined could be hurt economically. It is a very complicated situation, with powerful arguments on both sides. Nonetheless, coal switching can be at least part of the answer to the acid rain problem in some cases.

Coal can be "cleaned" (separated from its contaminating impurities) by crushing it and letting gravity help separate out impurities.

Coal Washing. Coal washing is the process of removing some of the sulfur and other impurities from coal before burning it. Some of the sulfur contained in coal is in the form of pyrites, which are heavy compounds. When crushed coal is rinsed with water and passed over several sizes of mesh

screens, much of the pyrite is washed out. This usually removes about 20 percent of the total sulfur contained in coal. The rest is tightly bonded to the coal and will separate only when the coal is burned.

Better Ways to Burn Coal

The coal industry is trying to find better ways to burn coal so that more heat is given out with less damage to the environment.

Coal liquefaction and gasification are extremely efficient processes that are being researched. Liquefaction converts the coal to a fluid state. It will probably be most useful as a petroleum substitute for the transportation industry. In the gasification process, coal reacts with oxygen at very high temperatures and produces a fuel that may be used as a substitute for natural gas. It is called SNG, for *synthetic natural gas*. These processes produce a lot less air pollution than using coal in its original form, but they also waste about 30 to 40 percent of the coal mined.

There are also several methods for making coal burn more efficiently. One of these is called fluidized-bed combustion. In this process, crushed coal is burned over a bed of limestone. The limestone "captures" much of the sulfur as the coal is burned, and thus sulfur dioxide emissions are almost completely eliminated. The limestone is usually disposed of in a landfill, which can cause problems.

Another way of reducing acid rain is by using "scrubbers" on smokestacks. This special equipment sprays lime into the smoke to remove the sulfur dioxide from the gases going up the stack. This multilevel scrubber keeps 90 percent of the sulfur from entering the air.

Another method is called ocean thermal-energy conversion. This method traps some of the heat that is otherwise wasted in the coal-burning process by vaporization and condensation. The word "ocean" is used because seawater was used in early versions of the process, but other types of liquids have since been substituted. Because it is a liquid process, the sulfur dioxide that is captured becomes sulfuric acid, which can be sold as a by-product of the process.

Cleaning the Emissions

Cleaning up emissions before they leave the smokestack and pollute the air is one of the major areas of research into prevention of acid rain.

Scrubbing Smoke. One of the most successful ways of cleaning up the smoke is to pass it through equipment called scrubbers. Scrubbers can remove as much as 95 percent of sulfur emissions, but they are also very expensive. Adding the scrubbing machinery to already existing coal-burning plants costs millions of dollars and takes lots of space. It is much less expensive when the machinery is included as part of the plan for new plants.

Scrubbing is officially called flue gas desulfurization. It works by injecting an alkaline substance, such as lime, into the smokestack of the coal-burning furnace. The scrubber is a huge hollow cylinder connected at one end to the boiler where coal is burned so that gases released by the burning go up into it. About halfway up the cylinder these gases meet liquid lime that is sprayed into the cylinder. The liquid lime and the sulfur from the gases mix, forming a sludge

that falls back to the bottom of the cylinder and is pumped out. The "scrubbed" gases continue up the cylinder and are expelled through the smokestack.

The alkaline-sulfur sludge is carried out separately. The sludge presents a new problem—what to do with it. In some cases it can be converted into a useful substance, such as gypsum, and sold to offset the costs of the scrubbing technology. But more often the sludge is chemically contaminated and is worthless.

In addition, the scrubbing process requires many employees to operate and maintain the equipment. Some of these employees have very difficult jobs, like spraying water on the sludge on outside conveyor belts in subzero weather to keep it moving. It is not a process without costs and difficulties, especially the sheer bulk of the waste sludge. But it seems to be one of the best ways to keep sulfur dioxide out of coal-burning emissions.

In Japan, scrubbers have been used extensively on coal-

Because power plants burn much of the coal that spews sulfur into the air, some power companies have built huge scrubbers to remove as much sulfur as possible from the smoke. The photo above shows six scrubbers attached to a smokestack, which is still under construction.

One of the best ways individuals can help prevent nitrogen oxides from contributing to acid rain is by using public transportation whenever possible.

burning plants. Even though energy consumption in that country has increased significantly, sulfur dioxide emissions have decreased thanks to the use of this technology.

Scrubbing is currently not as successful with nitrogen oxides. The process removes only about 30 percent from the emissions. A more efficient process using isocyanic acid to capture the nitrogen oxides is in the process of development. It is expected to remove up to 99 percent of the NO_x and leave only nitrogen and water as by-products.

Nitrogen Oxides. Controls that limit the emissions from automobiles are helping to reduce the amount of nitrogen oxides and hydrocarbons in the air. Emission-control devices such as catalytic converters are put on the exhaust systems of cars to keep impurities out of the air. Unfortunately, light trucks and minivans have not been required to have converters in the past and these are very popular vehicles. Also, some people have thought they were being clever when they disconnected their converters. They thought that they would save money by being able to use leaded gasoline, which was, for many years, cheaper than unleaded gasoline. But all those people did was continue to harm the environment.

More efficient engines that burn fuel other than gasoline are the best possibility for the future. Much more research needs to be done in this area.

The Role of Governments

Governments can encourage more industries to reduce emissions in a number of ways. One way is by passing and enforcing laws. Another is by levying taxes on emissions. In Japan, companies are taxed on their rate of emissions, thus encouraging reductions. In Sweden, industries that exceed certain standards are charged a heavy fee.

Legislation. Laws passed to reduce emissions usually focus on the condition of ambient air (the air people breathe) in specific areas. Such laws seldom deal with emissions that are transported hundreds of miles away, like acid rain.

In the United States, the Clean Air Act of 1970 is the most important law dealing with acid rain. It has been amended (changed) several times, most recently in 1990, to bring it up to date with the latest research and technologies. The law establishes maximum levels for various pollutants, including sulfur dioxide, in the air we breathe. It also calls for pollution controls on new coal-burning facilities. Most cities will have to meet these standards by 1995, but the most polluted, such as Los Angeles and New York City, will have until the year 2000.

But standards for new facilities alone won't do the job. Standards must be applied to existing plants as well. Power companies tend to use their old, polluting facilities more than the new, cleaner ones because the old ones appear to be cheaper to operate. But if the cost of damage to the environment is included, new, less-polluting operations seem less costly.

Protesters in Europe brought public attention to acid rain by mounting a huge banner on Nelson's Column in London.

Legislation requiring the use of pollution-control devices on cars—and the unleaded gasoline such devices require—has greatly reduced the pollutants in the air in many areas.

According to the EPA, during the 1970s and 1980s, there was a decrease of 95 percent in the use of lead in gasoline, which resulted in a 79 percent decrease in the amount of lead found in the blood of American citizens. Unfortunately, the United States continues to export large quantities of leaded gasoline to developing nations around the world. If leaded gasoline is bad for Americans, it is certainly bad for the rest of the world, too.

So far, legislation is not strong enough. Pollution levels in the air we breathe are often too high and very little is done about them. Many coal-burning companies continue to use old heavily polluting facilities rather than build new ones with costly pollution-control devices.

In addition to laws that do more to control emissions, we need laws requiring new products to be energy efficient and nonpolluting. For example, stricter standards for refrigerators, water heaters, and air conditioners could be set. In many cases, these appliances used to be more efficient than the new ones sold today. Thousands of megawatts of electricity could be saved, which would mean less fossil fuel burned and less emissions produced.

During the debate in 1990 on amending the Clean Air Act, Senate Majority Leader George J. Mitchell was asked if industry could survive with the restrictions placed on it by pollution-control measures. Mitchell replied, "Will the American people survive the failure to enact this bill?"

A Global Problem. The problem continues to plague countries around the world. Even many of the Third World countries of the Southern Hemisphere now have to deal with acid and toxic rain. The increased industry they need to strengthen their economies has also increased toxic emissions. Some cities in India, China, and Brazil are as heavily polluted as cities in Europe and North America.

The government standards for ozone levels in Mexico have been much more lenient than in the United States. Even so, "safe" levels are exceeded in Mexico City on as many as 300 days a year. Many city buses now use alternative fuels, but private cars, which don't, continue to increase in number.

FACT

Governments must decide how much air pollution is permissible and how much pollution can come from any single source. Then they must enforce these laws and penalize anyone who exceeds the limits.

Because the source of acid rain may not be within an affected nation's borders, the countries of the world must work together to solve the problem. International conferences have been held to share information on the subject and to encourage cooperation in reducing emissions. By signing a 1985 agreement, most of the countries of Europe joined the "30 Percent Club." That is, they agreed to reduce sulfur dioxide emissions by at least 30 percent by 1993. Some promised to cut sulfur dioxide emissions by 50 to 65 percent soon thereafter. It is up to all the countries involved to see that these reductions are made, to pressure the countries that don't make reductions, to monitor acid deposition to be sure that the reductions are great enough, and to further reduce sulfur dioxide and other toxic emissions as much as possible in the future.

The 30% Club	Agreed to Cut
Austria	50% by 1993
Belgium	50% by 1993
Bulgaria	30% by 1993
Canada	50% by 1994
Czechoslovakia	30% by 1993
Denmark	40% by 1995
East Germany	30% by 1993
Finland	50% by 1993
France	50% by 1990
Hungary	30% by 1993
Italy	30% by 1993
Liechtenstein	30% by 1993
Luxembourg	58% by 1990
Netherlands	50% by 1995
Norway	50% by 1994
Sweden	65% by 1995
Switzerland	30% by 1993
USSR	30% by 1993
West Germany	65% by 1993

The Role of Industry

Industries that are not willing to take pollution-control steps on their own must be strongly encouraged—forced, if necessary—to do so. But it is hoped that more and more companies will make changes willingly. After all, companies are run by people, and they have to live on this planet, too.

According to *Environmental Science and Technology Magazine*, industry spent $180 billion on emission controls between 1972 and 1985, with one-third of that being spent by electric utilities. That was a big step forward, showing that action can be taken to deal with this serious environmental problem. But much more can and should be done.

Co-generation. Besides burning fuel more efficiently and capturing as much of their emissions as possible, some industries can become more environmentally friendly and reduce the acid rain problem by using a process known as co-generation. Co-generation is the process of getting two uses—electricity and heat—from the burning of one fuel.

For example, the Dow Chemical plant near Sarnia, Ontario, produced steam in a boiler in the making of chemicals. There was often more steam produced than was

Some industrial processes create pollution that harms both the air and the water. Such pollution can be carried long distances, where it does further damage as it travels and when it lands.

needed, so the company installed equipment to convert the excess heat to electricity. That electricity now meets the needs of the entire plant. The company saves money, because it doesn't have to purchase electricity, and fossil fuels are not burned to produce that electricity.

Companies Taking Action. Some companies, like Dow, are doing their part to reduce pollution. By controlling toxic emissions, by efficient use of energy, and by producing environmentally friendly products, they are helping to save the Earth.

Other companies have not been so wise. Many opportunities have been lost by pollution creators to clean up their acts. But what's past is past. The important thing now is not to miss any more such opportunities to be better citizens of this planet.

As consumers we need to learn more about the companies that provide the products and services we use. We need to support the ones that are taking necessary steps to halt pollution and let the others know that we are not pleased with them.

The technology exists. It is expensive. It must be considered a part of the cost of doing business. If it means that we

This special power plant in California burns old tires as fuel. Tires are made of oil, a fossil fuel, yet they burn at such a high temperature that there is very little pollutant left to enter the atmosphere.

have to pay more for some products and services, we must be willing to do that for the sake of saving planet Earth. We also need to look for ways to make pollution control less expensive. And we have to remember that the expense of cleaning up is much, much greater.

This power plant in Germany burns waste materials to produce electricity and heats the nearby municipal swimming pool, all in one process.

Chapter 9

Taking Action

ACID RAIN IS SUCH A HUGE PROBLEM in terms of its global effects that you might think there is very little you can do about it.

But there are a number of significant things you can do. If we are going to save our environment, it is important that everyone helps out!

1. The first step is to begin some serious energy conservation. The average American uses more energy than a citizen of any other nation in the world— 8 $^1/_2$ times as much as a Canadian, 1 $^1/_2$ times as much as a Russian, 24 times as much as an Australian. We can and must cut down.

How many times have you been told to turn off the lights in a room or to shut off the TV? (Or are you the one who reminds other people?) Keeping electrical equipment running only when it is needed means less coal burned to produce electricity. And that can cut down on air pollution and save your family dollars at the same time.

2. Reduce the amount of driving you are responsible for. Even if you don't drive yet, you probably get many rides. Be as efficient about it as possible. Take public transportation or carpool with others. Rather than you and a friend each arriving somewhere in separate cars, take turns asking your parents to pick the other up. It can save your folks some driving, and it uses less gas. If you have a bike, use it! And there are probably many places you go to which you can walk.

3. Take up sports that don't require the use of fuel. For example, go cross-country skiing instead of snowmobiling. Use a rowboat or a sailboat instead of a motorboat or jet ski. Wind surfing can replace waterskiing. Using your body's energy instead of fossil fuel is lots better for your body, too.

4. Be an environment-conscious consumer. This means

This commuter in Santa Clara, California, is saving the environment in two ways: he uses public transportation to move long distances, and then completes his journey on his bicycle. The train has a space for riders to store their bikes.

making responsible choices about the products you buy. In the future, when you buy a car, choose a fuel-efficient one and make sure its pollution-control devices work. Be aware that some appliances and electric-powered toys are more energy conservative than others. Consider doing without so many electric gadgets. Even if they're battery-powered, the batteries must be disposed of. Send them for recycling.

5. Recycle as much as possible. Recycling reduces the amount of energy used to create new products and saves natural resources.

6. Learn as much as you can about acid rain and other environmental problems and tell other people what you have learned.

7. Write letters to companies that have good pollution-control records—and to those that don't. Speak up and be heard! It's our planet, after all—the only one we've got. Write and express your opinion to the state and national legislators who can make the laws that will protect our future world.

Writing Letters. In writing a letter to express your opinion on controversial issues, follow these seven tips:

1. Make your letter one page or less. Cover only one subject in each letter.

2. Introduce yourself and tell why you, personally, are for or against the issue.

3. Be clear and to the point.

4. Be specific on whether you want the person to vote "yes" or "no."

5. Write as an individual. The environmental group you belong to will have already let the legislator know its stand on the issue.

6. When you get a response, write a follow-up letter to re-emphasize your position and give your reaction to your legislator's comments.

7. Write again to thank your legislators if they vote the way you asked them to.

On issues concerning state legislation, or to express your opinion about actions taken by your state environmental or natural resources agency, you can write to:

Recycling all waste possible is important to solving the acid rain problem because it takes less fuel to recycle a material than it does to make a new one.

Your local, state, or provincial legislator. Check at your local library to discover his or her name.

The governor of your state or premier of your province. Write in care of your state or provincial capital.

The director of your state's department of natural resources or related environmental agency. Check your local library for the specific person and the address.

On issues concerning federal legislation or to express your opinion about actions taken by the federal government, you can write to:

Your two state senators. Check at your local library to discover their names.

    The Honorable _____
    U.S. Senate
    Washington, DC 20510

Your local congressman. Check at your local library to discover his or her name.

    The Honorable _____
    U.S. House of Representatives
    Washington, DC 20515

Your local provincial or federal member of Parliament. Check at your local library to discover his or her name.

    The Honorable _____
    House of Commons
    Ottawa, Ontario, Canada K1A 0A6

The President of the United States. He has the power to veto, or turn down, bills approved by the Senate and the House of Representatives as well as to introduce bills of his own. He also has final control over what the U.S. Environmental Protection Agency and other agencies do.

President _____
The White House
1600 Pennsylvania Avenue, NW
Washington, DC 20501
The Prime Minister of Canada.
The Honorable _____
House of Commons
Ottawa, Ontario, Canada K1A 0A6

Join Organizations

Many groups of people care about the prevention of acid and toxic rain and other air pollutants. They are constantly on the lookout for places where dangerous substances are emitted. They do their best to inform the general public about hazards to their health and what to do about them. Many organizations have local chapters.

The National Clean Air Coalition, 530 Seventh Street, SE, Washington, DC 20003, is made up of groups ranging from the American Lung Association to the League of Women Voters to the United Steelworkers of America. All the organizations in the coalition agree on at least one thing: we all have a right to breathe clean air.

The National Audubon Society, 801 Pennsylvania Ave., NE, Washington, DC 20003, has set up a Citizens Acid Rain Monitoring Network across the United States. Members of this organization have been sampling rain and recording the results since 1987. In this way, members find out if there is an acid rain problem in their area and can get involved in doing something about it.

The Acid Rain Foundation, 1410 Varsity Drive, Raleigh,

NC 27606, is a good source for information on this environmental problem.

The following organizations also play a major role in fighting to preserve our environment:

Alliance to Save Energy, 1725 K St., NW, Washington, DC 20006

American Forestry Association, 1516 P St., NW,Washington, DC 20036

Canadian Wildlife Federation, 1673 Carling Ave., Ottawa, Ontario, Canada K2A 3Z1

Center for Environmental Information, 99 Court Street, Rochester, NY 14604

Environmental Defense Fund, 1616 P St., NW, Washington, DC 20036

Greenpeace USA, 1436 U St., NW, Washington, DC 20009

National Wildlife Federation, 1400 16th St., NW, Washington, DC 20036

The Sierra Club, 730 Polk Street, San Francisco, CA 94109

World Wildlife Fund, 1250 24th St., NW, Washington, DC 20037, or 60 St. Clair Ave., E., Suite 201, Toronto, Ontario, Canada M4T 1N5

Worldwatch Institute, 1776 Massachusetts Ave., NW, Washington, DC 20036

Don't let anyone tell you that "pollution is the price of progress." Tell them that the price is too high. "Progress" that destroys the air we breathe, the water we drink, the food we eat, the animals we share the planet with, and the health of the children of the world isn't really progress, is it?

Yes, it is going to be expensive to reduce emissions. But the costs of *not* doing it are beyond imagining. These costs include the extinction of species after species of plant and animal life until entire ecosystems break down, until the planet Earth can no longer support life. Right now, the planet is crippled. It is up to us to heal it.

The problem of acid rain affects the land, the water, and the wildlife with which we share the planet. It is up to the human beings who created the problem to work to heal the Earth.

119

GLOSSARY

acid – a substance with a quantity of positively charged hydrogen ions; the more hydrogen ions, the stronger the acid. Acidic substances turn blue litmus paper red and are capable of dissolving some metals. An acid has a pH below 7.

acid deposition – the transferring of acid substances from the air to the ground or other surfaces; can be wet (rain, snow, sleet, fog) or dry (gases and tiny particles).

acid haze – minute particles of sulfuric and nitric acid that accumulate in the air, blocking sunlight, causing a dull-looking, hazy sky.

acid rain – precipitation that is higher than normal in acid content. Normal pH for rainfall is about 5; precipitation with a pH of less than 5 is generally accepted as acid rain. The term is often used to include all forms of wet acid deposition.

alkaline – see **base**.

aquatic – living in or having to do with water.

base – a substance that turns red litmus paper blue. Another word for *basic* is alkaline. Bases are the opposites of acids. A base has a pH above 7.

buffer – to neutralize (or attempt to neutralize) acid.

co-generation – the use of one quantity of fuel to produce both heat and electricity.

dioxin – a complex chemical substance found in petroleum-based herbicides and other chemical products that is suspected to cause cancer in humans.

ecosystem – a group of organisms, both plant and animal, that live within a specific environment with which they interact.

emissions – substances discharged into the air, generally as a result of a chemical process such as burning.

EPA – see **United States Environmental Protection Agency**

fossil fuels – coal, oil (petroleum), and natural gas, which were formed from the fossilized remains of ancient organisms. When fossil fuels are burned, they give off pollutants of several types.

gaseous – existing as a gas; not liquid or solid.

geothermal energy – "Earth heat." Geothermal energy is naturally occurring heat sources in the Earth, such as geysers and hot springs.

groundwater – water deep in the ground but above the underlying rock. In low-lying places, it forms lakes and ponds. At higher elevations, it is reached only by wells.

hydrocarbons – organic compounds that contain only the elements hydrogen and carbon. Benzene and methane are examples of hydrocarbons.

leaching – the removal of a soluble substance by a liquid, such as when nutrients are leached or washed from the soil by acid rain.

liming – the dumping of alkaline compounds, such as crushed limestone, into a lake or onto a field to neutralize acidity.

litmus paper – paper containing a powder made from a special lichen, used to determine whether a fluid substance is an acid or base. Red litmus paper turns blue in bases. Blue litmus paper turns red in acids.

neutralize – to use a base to change an acid (or an acid to change a base) into a substance that is neither basic nor acidic; to change the pH to approximately 7.

neutralizing capacity – the extent to which particular water or soil neutralizes acid; also called buffering capacity. Soil or water with high acid-neutralizing capability (ANC), contains lots of alkaline substances.

nitric acid – HNO_3, a highly corrosive liquid useful under controlled circumstances in a number of products such as fertilizer, explosives, and rocket fuel. When formed in the atmosphere, nitric acid can be very harmful to living organisms.

nitrogen oxide – NO_x, any of several colorless gases composed of nitrogen and oxygen.

osmoregulation – the process by which fish and other living organisms maintain the proper balance of gases, minerals, nutrients, etc., in their tissues.

ozone – O_3, a gas formed by a reaction between nitrogen oxides and hydrocarbons in the presence of sunshine. Suspected of causing damage to trees and crops and harming human health while in the lower atmosphere, ozone contributes to protecting life from ultraviolet radiation while in the upper atmosphere.

pH – an abbreviation for *potential hydrogen*, used as an indicator of the strength of an acid or base.

pH measuring paper – special paper for determining the strength (pH level) of an acid or base.

pH scale – the pH scale runs from 0 to 14, 0 being as strong as an acid can be, 14 being as strong as a base can be, and 7 being neutral.

precipitation – moisture falling to the Earth's surface as rain, snow, sleet, hail, or fog.

pyrites – a heavy metallic mineral containing sulfur, found loosely bonded to coal.

runoff – rainfall or snowmelt that is not absorbed by the soil, but which "runs off" the surface of the ground into sewage systems and surface waters.

secondary pollutants – chemical compounds such as ozone that are not present in initial emissions but which form from reactions between various emissions and the atmosphere.

sulfur dioxide – SO_2, a colorless gas composed of sulfur and oxygen, which is irritating to human lungs and contributes to the corrosion of metals.

sulfuric acid – H_2SO_4, a highly corrosive liquid useful under controlled circumstances in a number of products such as fertilizers, detergents, and explosives. When formed in the atmosphere, sulfuric acid can be very harmful to living organisms.

tallstacks – tall smokestacks built at many fossil-fuel burning sites during the 1970s in an effort to reduce local pollution, but which have tended to increase long-range transport of pollutants.

terrestrial – living on or having to do with the land.

toxic – harmful or dangerous; poisonous.

toxic rain – rainfall or other precipitation that contains toxic or harmful substances (such as lead or mercury) washed from the air with the rain. Sometimes includes the dry deposition of such toxic substances falling from the sky with ash or dust.

United States Environmental Protection Agency (EPA) – A federal government agency whose job it is to regulate factors of the environment and conditions that may be affecting it.

watershed – a region of land in which all rivers drain into one body of water, such as a lake.

INDEX

Bold number = illustration

PHOTO SOURCES

The Acid Rain Foundation, Inc.: 28 (both)
American Coal Foundation: 12 (both)
American Electric Power Service Corporation: 103
American Public Transportation Association: 15 (bottom left), 104, 114
Photo courtesy of American Ref-Fuel Company: 111
Photo by Kenneth Beland, United States Fish and Wildlife Service: 61
Ellis B. Cowling, North Carolina State University/The Acid Rain Foundation, Inc.: 47 (left)
S.C. Delaney/EPA: 15 (top left) 26, 30, 41, 63 (bottom), 115
Photo courtesy of The EPRI Journal: 39, 67, 96, 100, 101
Kelly Farris-Renner: 48
Hadley/Greenpeace: 106
Photo by Terry Haines, United States Fish and Wildlife Service: 46, 51, 54
Industry, Science and Technology, Canada, Photo, Ottawa, Ontario: 80
Industry, Science and Technology, Canada, Photo, Ste. Claire, Quebec: 78
Photo by Charles Jagoe, United States Fish and Wildlife Service: 58 (top left and right)
William Keller: 33, 40, 53
Lee and Weber/The Acid Rain Foundation, Inc.: 77
Dr. Gene Likens, Cornell University/The Acid Rain Foundation, Inc.: 58 (bottom)
Photographs courtesy of S.E. Lindberg/Oak Ridge National Laboratory: 14, 38, 43, 64
Martensen/Greenpeace: 84 (bottom)
Michigan Department of Natural Resources: 17 (bottom)
Courtesy Michigan Travel Bureau: 112

Milwaukee Public Museum: 10
The National Atmospheric Deposition Program/The Acid Rain Foundation, Inc.: 50 (left), 84 (top)
National Aeronautics and Space Administration: 17 (top)
National Oceanic and Atmospheric Admistration: 15 (top right), 36
National Park Service: 83 (both)
National Park Service photo by John Kauffmann: 21
National Park Service photo by M. Woodbridge Williams: 119
Northeast Sustainable Energy Association: 98 (right)
Dr. Lars Overrein, Norwegian Forest Research Institute/The Acid Rain Foundation, Inc.: 50 (right), 59 (all)
The Oxford Energy Company: 110
Roy F. Weston, Inc.: 47 (right)
Salt River Project: 15 (bottom right)
Mike Storey: 6, 66
UPI/Bettmann: 92
United States Department of Agriculture: 8, 9, 72 (both)
United States Department of Agriculture Forest Service: 44
United States Department of Agriculture Soil Conservation Service: 63 (top)
United States Department of Energy: 13, 24, 73, 91, 94
United States Fish and Wildlife Service: 56
United States Fish and Wildlife Service/Bill Thrune: 62
United States Fish and Wildlife Service Windpower, Inc., Livermore, California: 97
Wenkler/The Acid Rain Foundation, Inc.: 86 (both)
Weyerhauser: 70
Keith Winterhalder 31, 32, 34, 35
Wisconsin Department of Natural Resources: 109
World Bank Photo Library: 15 (center), 45, 98 (left)
Zindler/Greenpeace USA: 2

ABOUT THE AUTHOR

Eileen Lucas lives in southeastern Wisconsin with her husband and sons, Travis and Brenden. She graduated from Western Illinois University with a degree in Communications. She now works full-time writing nonfiction books for schoolchildren. In addition to another book in the SAVING PLANET EARTH series (*Water: A Resource in Crisis*), she has written biographies of Vincent Van Gogh and Jane Goodall, as well as a book on peaceful conflict solving.